I0407980

DISSIDENTS WHO HAVE SUFFERED FOR HUMAN RIGHTS IN CHINA: A LOOK BACK AND A LOOK FORWARD

HEARING

BEFORE THE

CONGRESSIONAL-EXECUTIVE COMMISSION ON CHINA

ONE HUNDRED FOURTEENTH CONGRESS

SECOND SESSION

DECEMBER 7, 2016

Printed for the use of the Congressional-Executive Commission on China

Available via the World Wide Web: http://www.cecc.gov

U.S. GOVERNMENT PUBLISHING OFFICE

23–081 PDF   WASHINGTON : 2017

For sale by the Superintendent of Documents, U.S. Government Publishing Office
Internet: bookstore.gpo.gov   Phone: toll free (866) 512–1800; DC area (202) 512–1800
Fax: (202) 512–2104   Mail: Stop IDCC, Washington, DC 20402–0001

CONGRESSIONAL-EXECUTIVE COMMISSION ON CHINA

LEGISLATIVE BRANCH COMMISSIONERS

House

CHRIS SMITH, New Jersey, *Chairman*
ROBERT PITTENGER, North Carolina
TRENT FRANKS, Arizona
RANDY HULTGREN, Illinois
DIANE BLACK, Tennessee
TIM WALZ, Minnesota
MARCY KAPTUR, Ohio
MICHAEL HONDA, California
TED LIEU, California

Senate

MARCO RUBIO, Florida, *Cochairman*
TOM COTTON, Arkansas
STEVE DAINES, Montana
JAMES LANKFORD, Oklahoma
BEN SASSE, Nebraska
DIANNE FEINSTEIN, California
JEFF MERKLEY, Oregon
GARY PETERS, Michigan

EXECUTIVE BRANCH COMMISSIONERS

CHRISTOPHER P. LU, Department of Labor
SARAH SEWALL, Department of State
STEFAN M. SELIG, Department of Commerce
DANIEL R. RUSSEL, Department of State
TOM MALINOWSKI, Department of State

PAUL B. PROTIC, *Staff Director*
ELYSE B. ANDERSON, *Deputy Staff Director*

(II)

CONTENTS

STATEMENTS

APPENDIX

PREPARED STATEMENTS

SUBMISSIONS FOR THE RECORD

DISSIDENTS WHO HAVE SUFFERED FOR HUMAN RIGHTS IN CHINA: A LOOK BACK AND A LOOK FORWARD

WEDNESDAY, DECEMBER 7, 2016

Congressional-Executive
Commission on China,
Washington, DC.

The hearing was convened, pursuant to notice, at 2:11 p.m., in Room HVC–210, Capitol Visitor Center, Hon. Christopher Smith, Chairman, presiding.

Also Present: Senator Rubio and Representatives Walz and Hultgren.

OPENING STATEMENT OF HON. CHRISTOPHER SMITH, A U.S. REPRESENTATIVE FROM NEW JERSEY; CHAIRMAN, CONGRESSIONAL–EXECUTIVE COMMISSION ON CHINA

Chairman SMITH. The Commission will come to order. Let me, first of all, say I am sorry for the lateness. There is a series of votes on the House floor. We just finished, so other Members should be streaming in.

Senator Marco Rubio and the other Senators also have a vote right now. So you never plan these things. I want to thank you for your patience, forbearance.

This has been another dark and difficult year for Chinese rights defenders and democracy activists and nobody knows that better than our distinguished witnesses at this table who have lived and suffered for their beliefs, for their convictions, and now others in like manner are suffering today in China. Under President Xi Jinping's version of the rule of law, the law is being used to more effectively curb freedom of expression, civil society, religious freedom, the forced abortion policy, and other fundamental rights.

Chinese courts have convicted rights activists and lawyers of "subversion of power" for simply seeking to represent religious groups, petitioners, and democracy activists. China's diverse religious communities, faced with even more restrictions, as new regulations, and "sinicization" campaign continues, will further politicize religious life and it leads to more repression.

In Hong Kong, mainland China's political interference and its abduction of booksellers threatens the rule of law and Hong Kong's promised autonomy, contributing to a growing climate of fear and insecurity. Internationally, China continues to push a relativistic vision and version of human rights, characterizing universal values as "Western" values that do not apply to the Chinese national situation. Even though what we espouse here and what others are pushing both within and from without China are all based on the Universal Declaration of Human Rights to which China and others have acceded to.

The next Administration faces major challenges in dealing with China. A new approach is needed that learns the lessons of the past and listens to those who have suffered prison and persecution to advance fundamental freedoms in China. The problem is that U.S. diplomacy is stuck with policies that no longer match—and maybe never did match—Chinese realities.

For the past two decades—or a little more than that—U.S. policy was based on the belief that China's growing prosperity would somehow bring political reforms and the rule of law; that trade matriculates into fundamental freedoms. Many of us argued from the beginning, including me and I am not the only one, going back to 1994, that it was a mistake when President Bill Clinton delinked most-favored-nation status with human rights, and by doing so said that profits trump fundamental freedoms and fundamental rights.

That was the beginning in my opinion. The Chinese took the measure of the United States and said they care more about money than they do about values. But that is not the case, certainly on this Commission, and that is a bipartisan belief that we have.

During those times, we focused on integrating China into the international system, ignoring clear evidence that China, under the Communist Party's leadership, would play by its own rules.

China has not become a "responsible stakeholder" in the international system as predicted. I would note parenthetically that I also chair the Africa, Global Health, Global Human Rights subcommittee; frequently travel to Africa and other parts of the world on human rights missions, and I could tell you the bad governance model that they promulgate is being accepted by certain autocratic governments, if not dictatorships, on those continents. So they are not acting as a responsible stakeholder.

To the contrary, despite decades of remarkable economic growth, Beijing's leaders are increasingly dismissive of "Western influence" and outright hostile to both free societies and democratic capitalism.

A strategy of engagement through trade, investment, and people-to-people exchanges has not lead to a freer China and remains cold comfort to China's repressed human rights lawyers, religious and ethnic minority groups, journalists, and civil society leaders. The United States must recognize that China's internal repression drives its external aggression and develop new policy approaches that intertwine our principles and interests in the pivotal Asia-Pacific region.

Working with the Congress, the next Administration should be prepared to bolster U.S. strategic advantages in the Asia-Pacific region. This will mean improving military readiness, insisting on a freer and fairer trade, strengthening relations with regional partners, and making more robust commitments to advancing democratic institutions, human rights, and the rule of law.

This last point will require the United States to push China to embrace greater transparency and a better adherence to universal standards. It will require the next Administration to shine a bright light on human rights abuses and level meaningful sanctions in response to these abuses which I say with great sadness, that this Administration, the Obama Administration, has not done for the last eight years. The United States must also find ways to support China's reformers, their dissidents, and its champions of liberty and the rule of law.

The bipartisan Congressional-Executive Commission on China [CECC], which Senator Rubio and I cochair, recently issued its 2016 Annual Report with specific recommendations for ways to pursue human rights and the rule of law within U.S.-China relations.

This report is the "gold standard" of human rights reports on China. I want to publicly commend the CECC staff for their Herculean efforts in producing this important report. It is a big task and we appreciate their hard work. The report should be required reading for Members of Congress interested in things related to China, journalists writing on China, and for Administration officials looking to develop strategies to engage with China.

The need for a principled and consistent American leadership is more important than ever, as China's growing economic clout, and persistent diplomatic efforts, have succeeded in dampening global criticism of its escalating repression and failures to adhere to universal standards. We owe a new approach to the great people like Liu Xiaobo, who continues as a Noble Peace Prize winner to sit in prison, people like Gao Zhisheng, and the thousands of others suffering as prisoners of conscience.

Now, we owe it to future generations of Americans, whose security and prosperity will depend on a U.S.-China relationship that is open and transparent, free of censorship and persecution, based on adherence to universal standards, and, hopefully, increasingly democratic.

It is my honor to turn to Cochair Senator Marco Rubio.

STATEMENT OF HON. MARCO RUBIO, A U.S. SENATOR FROM FLORIDA; COCHAIRMAN, CONGRESSIONAL–EXECUTIVE COMMISSION ON CHINA

Cochairman RUBIO. Thank you, Mr. Chairman, and I want to thank all of the witnesses gathered here today. This is an impressive group of men and women who have important stories to share about their own personal suffering and that of their family members and associates at the hands of both the Chinese Government and the Chinese Communist Party.

Their experiences must not be viewed in isolation, but rather they are representative of untold numbers of other Chinese, Tibetans, and Uyghurs who daily face repression at the hands of their own government.

Today I joined our Chairman, Representative Smith, in sending a letter to the Chinese Ambassador to raise our concern and seek additional information about a spate of detentions involving prominent Chinese human rights advocates, as well American citizen Sandy Phan-Gillis who has been arbitrarily detained for 21 months now. I submit a copy of that correspondence for the record.

Before going any further, I would also like to take a moment at
this hearing, the last CECC hearing of the 114th Congress, to recognize Chairman Smith for his capable and principled leadership
of the Commission. He is an unrelenting advocate for human rights
and rule of law everywhere in the world, especially in China, and
I look forward to continuing to partner with him in the new Congress, because as today's testimony will no doubt make clear, the
mandate and the mission of this Commission remains as vital as
ever.

The Commission, as you just heard a moment ago, recently released its Annual Report and it painted an undeniably bleak picture regarding the deterioration of human rights and the rule of
law in China, with especially grave consequences for civil society,
religious believers, human rights lawyers, and labor activists. Since
the Report's release in October of this year, those abuses have continued apace in the last two months.

As the Report documents and as news stories from the last several weeks underscore, Beijing has become increasingly brazen in
exerting its extraterritorial reach. This was especially true in the
outrageous abductions of the Hong Kong booksellers last year, including Swedish national Gui Minhai, who is still being held by
Chinese authorities at an undisclosed location.

And now more recently in China's unprecedented intervention in
Hong Kong's legal system in the cases surrounding two democratically elected politicians who won seats in the Legislative Council
on platforms calling for democratic self-determination for Hong
Kong. The ripple effects of this ruling are not fully known yet as
the Hong Kong Government has now taken additional steps tar-
geting opposition lawmakers. This is gravely concerning and something which the Commission, and the Congress, will be watching
closely in the coming year especially as it relates to the Hong Kong
Policy Act.

Returning to the focus of today's hearing, we are at a critical
juncture in U.S.-China relations, and there is much wisdom to be
gleaned, for the incoming administration, from dissident voices.

December will mark 15 years since China gained entry into the
World Trade Organization. It is past time to take stock of our approach and recognize that despite what proponents at the time believed would happen, China has in fact used the international rules-
based system to fuel vast economic growth, while further restricting freedom and increasing repression.

Quite simply, many of the principles which have undergirded
U.S.-China relations during Democrat and Republican administrations alike in recent decades have simply not yielded the desired
outcomes. A perennial critique from those who care about human
rights issues has been that the U.S. foreign policy apparatus risks
ghettoizing human rights concerns, only giving them the prominence they merit during infrequent, and often ineffective, human
rights dialogues and then relegating these issues to the sidelines
in high-level bilateral engagement.

The Obama Administration struggled to integrate human rights
issues at the highest levels sending unmistakable signals early on,
as was famously reported during then Secretary Clinton's inaugural trip to China in 2009 that human rights issues, "can't inter-

fere with the global economic crisis, the global climate change crisis, and the security crisis."

Words have consequences. Mid-level appointees at the State Department and elsewhere take them to heart. As such, it will be critical, during the early days of the new administration, for the Secretary and other senior diplomats to put down markers on these issues which are of central importance not only to the Chinese people, but to U.S. national interests. For as history has shown us, where rule of law fails to take root, where human rights abuses are committed with impunity, where international obligations are violated, the United States should not expect to find a responsible global stakeholder.

I look forward to hearing from our witnesses on this important topic. Today's hearing was scheduled to coincide with the commemoration of Human Rights Day this weekend, and also with the sixth anniversary of the awarding of the Nobel Peace Prize to Chinese dissident and writer Liu Xiaobo—an honor that he has not been able to rightfully claim given that still today he languishes unjustly in prison, serving an 11-year sentence handed down for his essays criticizing the Chinese Government.

The United States must commit anew to standing with China's reformers and dissidents, embracing their aspirations and consistently pressing the Chinese Government and its Communist Party to respect basic human rights and uphold the rule of law. It is my hope that this new administration will appoint an ambassador to China that reflects these priorities, not simply someone that is going there to catch up with old friends.

I look forward to today's testimony and to today's policy recommendations.

Thank you, Mr. Chairman, and just as a note, the Senate is in the midst of a series of votes. I know it is shocking the Senate is voting today. I am going to take my second vote and try to get back here as quickly as possible. Thank you, Chairman.

Chairman SMITH. I want to thank the Cochair for his leadership over the last two years, and really over the entirety of his tenure in the U.S. Senate on behalf of human rights everywhere, including and especially in China. Next Congress, God willing, you will serve as Chair. The Commission could not be in better hands. You are just an extraordinary leader.

I would like to now yield to Mr. Hultgren.

[The letter appears in the appendix.]

STATEMENT OF HON. RANDY HULTGREN, A U.S. REPRESENTATIVE FROM ILLINOIS

Representative HULTGREN. It is so good to be with all of you. I especially want to thank our wonderful Cochairmen, Congressman Smith and Senator Rubio, two people who could not be more passionate and more effective at fighting for the value of every single person, no matter where they are.

As I look out in the audience, truly we are among heroes. I want to thank you. You have lived your lives fighting for freedom, fighting for those who are being persecuted, being imprisoned, and we are so grateful that through you, we are able to make sure that their voices are heard, that no one is forgotten, and that no country, or leader, or person is left unaccountable for unacceptable actions.

So this is appropriate, certainly to look back on what has happened over the last few years, some successes, but also somethings that did not happen that should have happened, and to take that and to look forward to what can we do next. It is my commitment, along with the Cochairmen and other members of this Commission, to say that this is our responsibility.

There is opportunity, I think, in a new year and a new administration to make sure that, again, no one is forgotten, no voice is left unheard. My hope, my prayer, my commitment is to do every- thing that I can to make sure that we have that kind of account- ability and that we are holding other nations accountable; that we are doing all that we can to say that every person deserves to be treated with respect, with dignity, and with the ability to pursue their dreams, their religion, and their passions that is their right.

So thank you. Thank you Chairman Smith. Thank you for your incredible work, and thank you all for being here today.

Again, I appreciate the work that has been done, but even more so, looking forward to greater impact that we can have coming into the new year.

Chairman SMITH. Thank you, Randy, very much. Thank you for your leadership as well.

I would like to invite to the witness table our other three panelists. We have seven extraordinary women and men who have stood up for human rights in China, most of whom have spent considerable time in prison on behalf of their core convictions, and belief in human rights and religious freedom.

I would like to now begin introducing them one-by-one, and then invite you to present your testimony.

We will begin with Mr. Penpa Tsering who is the Representative of the Office of Tibet in Washington, and a member of the Tibetan Parliament. During his student days, he served as the General Secretary of both the Tibetan Freedom Movement and Nigerian Tibet Friendship Association.

Later, he served as General Secretary of the Central Executive Committee in Do-mey. He then worked as executive director of the Tibetan Parliamentary and Research Centre in New Delhi before being sworn in as the speaker of the 14th Tibetan Parliament in 2008. During the 15th Tibetan Parliament-in-exile in 2011, he again held the speaker's post. So thank you, Mr. Speaker, for being here.

We will then hear from Dr. Yang Jianli who is president of Initiatives for China/Citizen Power for China. Dr. Yang is a scholar and democracy activist internationally recognized for his efforts to promote democracy in China. He has been involved in the pro-democracy movement in China since the 1980s and was forced to flee China in 1989 after the Tiananmen Square massacre.

In 2002, Dr. Yang returned to China to support the labor movement and was imprisoned by Chinese authorities for alleged espionage and illegal entry. Following his release in 2007, he founded Initiatives for China, a non-governmental organization that promotes China's peaceful transition to democracy.

We will then hear from Mr. Chen Guangecheng, a Chinese legal advocate and extraordinary activist. Mr. Chen is from rural China where he advocated on behalf of people with disabilities and exposed and challenged abuses of population control and defended women—as well as their children—from forced abortion and forced sterilization.

Mr. Chen was imprisoned for his activism for four years, followed by an extra two years of extrajudicial confinement at his home. Chen Guangcheng escaped in 2012, in an escape that still defies imagination, how he was able to pull that off, then came to the United States with his family.

In addition to his position as a distinguished visiting fellow in the Institute for Policy Research and Catholic Studies at Catholic University, Mr. Chen is a senior distinguished fellow in human rights at the Witherspoon Institute, and also advisor to the Lantos Foundation for Human Rights and Justice.

This Commission, parenthetically, had four hearings on his behalf during that crisis. We are so glad he is free today.

We will then hear from Pastor Bob Fu who was a leader in the 1989 democracy movement in Tiananmen Square and later became a house church pastor. In 1996, authorities arrested and imprisoned Pastor Fu and his wife for their work.

After their release, they escaped to the United States, and in 2002, he founded ChinaAid Association. ChinaAid monitors and reports on religious freedom in China and provides a forum for discussions among experts in religion, law, and human rights.

Pastor Fu is frequently interviewed by media outlets around the world, has been before the European Parliament and the United Nations, and has been a particularly effective advisor to me and others, especially during Chen Guangeheng's crisis, but also on religious freedom. When Frank Wolf and I made our way on one of many trips to China, right before the Olympics in this case, we were in constant contact with Bob Fu as to which house pastors we might be able to meet with. So again, I want to thank him for his counsel and insight then.

Then we will hear from Wei Jingsheng, a longtime leader of the opposition against the Chinese Government dictatorship. He was sentenced to jail twice for a total of more than 18 years due to his democracy activism, including a groundbreaking and well-publicized essay he wrote in 1978, "The Fifth Modernization: Democracy."

After his exile to the United States in 1997—and I remember meeting him in Beijing when he was let out—one time, he was such a high-value political prisoner that the Chinese dictatorship thought that if they let out one man to get the Olympics for Beijing—this was the one that was held later on, this would have been Olympics 2000—they let Wei Jingsheng out. Then when the Olympics did not go their way, they rearrested him and tortured him. He is an incredible, incredible man, president of both the Wei Jingsheng Foundation and the Asia Democracy Alliance. I remem- ber meeting with him during that short respite when he was out of prison in Beijing, and he told me—and I tell everybody that I can ever meet with, particularly on this Commission, that one of his pieces of advice to us was that when you kowtow, when you placate, and treat with weakness the dictatorship in China, they beat the prisoners more. But when you are predictable, and tough, and transparent, and lay down clearly what you want to accomplish as a U.S. Government or Western power, they then respond and they beat the prisoners less.

We will then hear from Rebiya Kadeer who is a prominent human rights advocate and leader of the Uyghur people. She is the mother of 11 children. She spent six years in a Chinese prison for standing up to the authoritarian Chinese Government.

Before her arrest in 1999, she was a well-known Uyghur businesswoman. Ms. Kadeer has been actively campaigning for human rights for the Uyghur people since her release from prison in 2005.

She has been nominated for the Nobel Peace Prize several times. Despite Chinese Government efforts to discredit her, Rebiya Kadeer remains a pro-democracy Uyghur leader and heads the World Uyghur Congress, which represents the collective interest of Uyghurs around the world.

We will then hear from Danielle Wang, who was born in Beijing. Danielle Wang began practicing the exercise of meditation known as Falun Gong in her youth with her father, Wang Zhiwen.

In 1998, she moved to America for her studies. The following year, the Chinese Communist Party began its persecution of the Falun Gong practitioners. This put her father in prison and set her on a path for calling for help in the hopes of rescuing him for the next 17 years. He was released in 2014, but was denied exit from China when Danielle and her husband attempted to bring him to the United States in August 2016.

A very, very incredible group of leaders. I would like to now turn to Mr. Tsering to begin the testimony.

STATEMENT OF PENPA TSERING, REPRESENTATIVE OF HIS HOLINESS THE DALAI LAMA, OFFICE OF TIBET, WASHINGTON, DC

Mr. TSERING. Thank you Chairman Smith, Senator Rubio, and Congressman Hultgren for providing me this opportunity. This is my first testimony before the Commission after assuming the responsibility of the Representative of His Holiness the Dalai Lama and the Central Tibetan Administration.

I think this testimony is very timely because it is just before the International Human Rights Day, and also when you are going through a transition to a new administration at the helm of affairs in your country.

Following the results of your presidential election, His Holiness the Dalai Lama has written both to President-elect Donald Trump and to Secretary Clinton and has expressed his wish to meet them. I am sure the President-elect and Secretary Clinton will meet with His Holiness as American presidents have done in the past.

His Holiness the Dalai Lama and the Tibetan people are very concerned about the well-being of the Nobel Laureate, Liu Xiaobo, and demand his immediate release from incarceration.

As I present the case of Tibet before you, we Tibetans stand with Chinese, Uyghur, and Falun Gong friends who are represented here and also our Southern Mongolian friends who are, unfortunately, not represented here. We all suffer the same fate under the repressive Communist Government of the People's Republic of China.

While completely endorsing the findings and recommendations of the 2016 Annual Report of the Congressional-Executive Commission on China, I wish to briefly touch on the following points.

Religious freedom. Having to seek the PRC Government's approval for recognition of reincarnated Lamas is the ultimate political tool to undermine existing Buddhist religious practices. Just as is the case of the Chinese appointed Panchen Lama, and even though the present Dalai Lama has not been included in the list of so-called living Buddhas, the Communist government wants to be responsible for the reincarnation of the 14th Dalai Lama and they said it is an important issue concerning sovereignty and security of the nation.

There are many cases, but the ongoing destruction of Larung Gar, the biggest center of Buddhists learnings, not only for Tibetans, but also to scores of Chinese and repatriation of thousands of monks and nuns from the center forced to pledge never, ever to return is a case in point as to how China views religious freedom in Tibet.

Freedom of movement. Apart from the enormous restrictions on Tibetans to move from one part of Tibet to another, particularly into or out of Tibetan autonomous regions, Tibetans face tightening control to travel abroad. Tibetans who have obtained passports are being recalled. Tibetans who are already in India to receive the Kalachakra teachings from His Holiness the Dalai Lama in January 2017, have been ordered to return home before the end of December or face consequences. This includes denial of visas to Tibetan Americans to travel to Tibet.

The use of counterterrorism as a tool to control Tibetans and branding allegiance to the Dalai Lama as separatists are the four things I want to outline.

The diplomatic and political actions that have worked in the past:

Number 1. Presidential meeting with His Holiness the Dalai Lama.

Number 2. Appointment and the role of Special Coordinator for Tibet.

Number 3. Hearings and reports of the Commissions.

Number 4. Financial aid.

Number 5. Bills and resolutions.

Number 6. Congressional and State Department visits to Tibet and Dharamsala.

Suggestions to the new Administration and the Congress:

Number 1. As an integral part of U.S. policy on China, the United States should play a pivotal role in highlighting the human rights situation in China, Tibet, Xinjiang, and Southern Mongolia.

Number 2. The United States should advocate for the release of all political prisoners, including the Panchen Lama and Liu Xiaobo.

Number 3. The new Administration should implement U.S.-Tibetan Policy Act of 2002, including early appointment of a senior level State Department Special Coordinator for Tibet.

Number 4. The Administration should impress on China the need to establish a U.S. Consulate in Lhasa.

Number 5. Preserve and increase economic, educational, and humanitarian funding for Tibet, including radio broadcasts.

Number 6. The incoming president should meet with His Holiness the Dalai Lama at the earliest opportunity in keeping with precedence.

Number 7. The Administration should monitor misuse of counterterrorism in Tibet.

Number 8. The Administration and the Congress should urge the Chinese Government to resume dialogue with the representative of His Holiness the Dalai Lama without preconditions.

Number 9. The Administration and the Congress should emphasize to the Chinese leaders the need to teach in the Tibetan language.

Number 10. The Administration and the Congress should raise discriminatory policies of the PRC toward Tibetans in matters relating to religious freedom and freedom of movement.

Number 11. The Congress should support and adopt the Reciprocal Access to Tibet Bill to promote access to U.S. officials, journalists, and citizens into Tibet, Uyghur, and other minority nationalities.

Number 12. The Congress should organize more bipartisan, bicameral visits to Tibet and Dharamsala.

Thank you Chairman, Representative Chris Smith and Cochair, Senator Marco Rubio for the opportunity.

Chairman SMITH. Mr. Speaker, thank you so very much for your testimony and for your very specific recommendations, because all of this will be given to the next Administration. So thank you. This is a very important set of recommendations you have made.

Dr. Yang?

[The prepared statement of Mr. Tsering appears in the appendix.]

STATEMENT OF YANG JIANLI, INITIATIVES FOR CHINA/ CITIZEN POWER FOR CHINA

Mr. YANG. Mr. Chairman, I want to first thank you for your leadership and your moral courage and—in speaking out on human rights—so consistently and persistently, even when it is not always easy or convenient to do so. Thank you so much, Mr. Chairman.

By any standard, America's China policy has been a failure for the past three decades. The primary cause of the failure has been a fundamental misunderstanding of China's strategic objective, along with an inability on the part of the United States to respond to it with strategic and moral clarity.

Regime security is the number one concern for China's Communist Party. It wants to maintain a permanent rule in China, replace Western capitalism with socialism with Chinese characteristics and substitute its so-called civilization in the place of democracy.

The Trump Administration must take a different approach in dealing with the Chinese regime by returning to American values by focusing the foreign policy, then by striking directly at the vulnerable spots of the regime to enable a democratic transition. A democratic China will avoid inevitable conflict with the United States and assure a long-lasting peace in the region and in the world.

I recommend the following specific actions for the next administration.

Number 1. Use the U.S. market as leverage and threaten to withdraw China's permanent trade status unless serious improvements are made in the areas of human rights, political reform, and demilitarization of the South and East China Seas. Link continued progress on all three to all future relations, including trade. Deny foreign tax credits to companies that invest in the localities with gross human rights violations, and other similar measures to address the unfairness of one-way free trade that is resulting in China's huge trade surplus of $3 trillion with a resulting loss of millions of American jobs—all of which will not only bring back jobs from China, but allow the United States to take the moral high ground.

Number 2. Use Taiwan and Hong Kong as leverage. Modify the Taiwan Relations Act and the six assurances to reflect a full democratic country status and affirm its legitimacy by allowing Taiwan to be a normal member of the international community. Support Hong Kong's struggle for universal suffrage by making it a major bilateral issue with China.

Number 3. Use Japan as leverage. Encourage Japan to take the lead in promoting democracy in the Asia Pacific and return it to a normal status of a great power.

Number 4. Use the Chinese regime's lack of legitimacy and moral standing as leverage, engaged with the democratic forces in China, the Chinese, Tibetans, Uyghurs, Falun Gong Practitioners, Christians, representative of this panel as a new level by passing the China Democracy Act to ensure all U.S. Government agencies are resolute and consistent in advancing a democracy agenda when engaging with China.

And by passing China's Defense of Human Rights and Civil Society Act, a China-specific Magnitsky-like legislation that would ban travel and freeze the assets of Chinese human rights abusers. And pass the act to rename the plaza in front of the Chinese Embassy after imprisoned Nobel Laureate Dr. Liu Xiaobo.

Number 5. Use the UN human rights mechanism as leverage because both the Chinese Government and its people regard the United Nations as a legitimate world-governing authority, and the Chinese Government has taken the United Nations as the stage on which it seeks to compete with the United States to build a bi-polar world order in its own way. The Trump Administration must strengthen the U.S. leadership role in forming an alliance of democracies to collectively confront China on human rights issues.

Thank you.

Chairman Smith. Dr. Yang, thank you very much for your testimony and recommendations. As usual, you have been a great leader.

I would now like to ask Mr. Chen Guangcheng to present his testimony.

[The prepared statement of Mr. Yang appears in the appendix.]

STATEMENT OF CHEN GUANGCHENG, CHINESE LEGAL ADVOCATE; DISTINGUISHED VISITING FELLOW, INSTITUTE FOR POLICY RESEARCH AND CATHOLIC STUDIES, CATHOLIC UNIVERSITY OF AMERICA

Mr. Chen. Thank you. Greetings to the Chair people, to all the human rights Congressional representatives. Ladies and gentlemen, hello.

In China, people know me as the "barefoot lawyer." Despite having no formal training as a lawyer, I did the work of a lawyer, bringing officials to court and asking that the party respect China's own Constitution and laws. As a result, I endured seven years of kidnappings, house arrest, secret detention, and imprisonment.

After I was let out of prison, my family and I were put under illegal house arrest and conditions even worse than prison, including torture, until I finally escaped.

My own experience tells me that one should not hold out any hope in the Communist Party. This is a fascist regime that destroys the essential goodness of humanity.

The Communist Party has been persecuting its own people for years.

Last year it began the infamous 709 Crackdown, persecuting human rights defenders and lawyers, torturing people and implicating family members by association. Some attorneys and activists in detention have been forced to make confessions of guilt in the state-controlled media, and have subsequently been sentenced to prison.

But some, like Li Heping, Li Chunfu, Wang Quanzhang, and Xie Yang, and other attorneys refuse to admit guilt, and hence continue to be held illegally. Two weeks ago, Attorney Xie Yang was tortured by prison police, and Attorney Jiang Tianyong has been disappeared. Activists Huang Qi and Liu Feiyue have been taken by public security. Countless netizens have been blocked online, and their speech censored.

Under Party control, the Chinese people have long lived in a state of suffering and fear. It should be clear that Communist authoritarian control is the enemy of humanity. We must put a stop to its destruction of humanity's civilized values.

On the other hand, America is a great nation that truly stands out in its commitment to universal values. There is simply no way to compare the United States and China on this front. Hence, America must be a model for human rights, and a leader in the global push to democracy. The American system has the strongest immunity against corruption, and the greatest capability for correcting its mistakes.

Democracy, freedom, and human rights are America's founding principles. After many injurious years of appeasement and self-belittling, the time has come for the United States to reinvigorate its core values and to protect universal human rights.

I would like to make the following recommendations to the incoming Administration and Congress regarding human rights:

Number 1. Correct the mistaken policy of separating trade from human rights. Human rights are like clean water, clean food, and clean air—they are an indispensable part of life, and cannot be separated from anything we do.

The essence of the policy of separating trade and human rights is to focus solely on making money, without care to justice or ethics. In addition, the reality is that a country with strong human rights and rule of law is a better business partner for American companies.

Number 2. In its position as a global leader, the United States should express a position of leader support for the universal values of freedom, democracy, and human rights.

When a dictatorial regime uses force to suppress its people, the United States should act decisively to stop it. In addition, we should reconsider NATO's function, to transform NATO from a hedgehog quill to a heroic sword.

Number 3. Prevent human rights abusing officials from entering the United States. Investigate and where illegality is found, freeze the U.S. assets of Communist Party officials.

Number 4. Prevent the Communist Party from infiltrating U.S. academia, media, and other institutions.

Number 5. Demand that the Chinese Communist Party respect the UN International Treaty on Human Rights. Change the policy of speaking with the CCP [Chinese Communist Party] on issues of human rights behind closed doors, otherwise we will continue the useless conversations we have now.

Number 6. Ensure reciprocity of visas for journalists, and prevent the CCP from using visas to punish journalists who expose the crimes of the party.

Number 7. Invest in tools to get past Internet blocking mechanisms, to assist those who seek freedom in getting past the Great Firewall [Internet Berlin Wall]. Establish direct communication with the Chinese people, instead of just with the party.

Number 8. Establish international, collaborative mechanisms to prevent the Chinese Communist Party from persecuting its own people internally, and from breaking down international procedures externally.

Great nations have great responsibility. In Chinese there is an ancient saying: "Bring out the best and eliminate the worst under heaven." This should be the principle to follow.

As long as we join together, we can banish dictatorships, and make the world a better place.

Thank you.

Chairman SMITH. Mr. Chen, thank you very much for your eloquent statement. I would note that we have had—I have chaired 61 Congressional hearings on human rights in China. One was about you, four were with you when you spoke Chinese, and this

is the first time you have presented your testimony in English.
[Laughter.]

So, I thank you for that.

Mr. CHEN. Thank you.

Chairman SMITH. Bob Fu, our next speaker, was the one who
translated when you called in from your hospital bed in Beijing and
got you on the phone through some mysterious way I will never understand, but I would like to now yield to Pastor Bob Fu for his
testimony.

[The prepared statement of Mr. Chen appears in the appendix.]

STATEMENT OF BOB FU, FOUNDER AND PRESIDENT, CHINAAID ASSOCIATION

Mr. FU. Thank you, Mr. Chairman, thank you Congressman
Hultgren for your leadership, too. Thank you Cochairman Rubio for
the leadership.

Mr. Chairman, your persistency, perseverance, and constant attention on the human rights, religious freedom, and rule of law
globally, including my motherland, China, has, I think, already
made a lot of differences. Sometimes, we have some setbacks, but
I do think ultimately we will see a free and democratic, constitu-
tional China.

As my other distinguished friends and witnesses have already
said, we can pretty clearly see that today's China, the human
rights situation, and the situation on religious freedom and rule of
law should be recognized as the worst, perhaps, since the Cultural
Revolution.

Just to give you two latest illustrations, as my friend, Chen
Guangcheng, just mentioned, just barely 16 days ago a friend,
prominent human rights lawyer Jiang Tianyong, went missing and
presumably was kidnapped based on his past experiences, for visiting a family member of another imprisoned human rights lawyer,
Xie Yang.

Mr. Jiang Tianyong—remember in 2009, when I organized a rule
of law delegation with a group of human rights lawyers to the U.S.
Congress, and it was you, Mr. Chairman and Mr. Wolf, who actually organized two congressional hearings. I still remember when
we asked those fellow human rights lawyers and defenders who
were willing to really testify for two hearings: one on the rule of
law in China; one on the forced abortion and forced sterilization in
China.

Attorney Jiang Tianyong attended and testified twice. That really takes courage to do that. Today is the 16th day he is missing.

So I hope you could really exercise your leadership and continue
to push for his freedom. I want to recognize that Mr. Jiang
Tianyong's wife, Ms. Jin Bianling—I invited her to be here today,
really to witness this, and she is here today behind me. Ms. Jin
Bianling is here.

So we just visited the State Department and also the Minority
Leader, Nancy Pelosi. We hope that Mr. Jiang Tianyong's whereabouts could be, at least, revealed, if not freed. But he has committed nothing wrong, just the visiting of fellow family members of
human rights lawyers.

Another example—on November 29, just barely a week ago, another human rights and democracy leader, Mr. Peng Ming. He was suddenly declared dead by the prison authority after he was kidnapped from Burma as an American refugee and permanent resident and was sentenced to life in prison. So, for the last 12 years, he has been suffering imprisonment in China, and suddenly he was declared dead.

The government even confiscated his death certificate. His three children, who are all American citizens; several of them actually testified and met with you, like Lisa Peng, and they live in Cleveland, Ohio. They want to visit Peng Ming's funeral; and to bring his ashes back and his belongings. Yet, the day before yesterday, the Chinese Embassy and Consulate rejected their visa application even to visit their dead father.

So these are just the latest examples to show that really the situation is becoming very worrisome. I think it is time to have a major paradigm shift in the whole approach to the China policy in the next administration. The so-called laid on the back, or behind, or acquired diplomacy is nothing but a real miserable failure.

Here are just a few of my recommendations. Besides the recommendations, I really agree with the previous speakers on the— I think to help pass the global Magnitsky Act, to hold those human rights and religious freedom abusers and the corrupted officials accountable.

Another one I agree with is to really develop and push down the 21st century Berlin Wall, the Internet firewall. The other four, I would just very briefly mention that I want to encourage the Trump Administration officials and President-elect Trump to really—to not only raise these human rights abuse cases behind closed doors, but really, more importantly, to raise them publicly.

Second, I think it is time to use a multifaceted approach on human rights and religious freedom. The so-called annual Human Rights Dialogue is just nothing but a waste of time and taxpayers' money and should be abolished. I think human rights should be on the center and front. Overall, our strategy, no matter business, economic policy, strategic dialogue, this should be on the frontline.

Third, I encourage the incoming Trump Administration to adopt a concerted, internationally coordinated effort by working jointly with our allies in Europe and other regions. I think the release of imprisoned lawyer Zhang Kai and Pastor Wen Xiaowu were good examples—showing a concerted, coordinated effort globally could produce real fruit.

Fourth and finally, I think to really—this is important that the United States should unequivocally condemn the Chinese brutal violation of international laws by overstepping their own nation's boundaries to kidnap and detain citizens, I think, as Chairman Smith just mentioned in his opening remarks. The dissidents, like Jiang Yefei and Dong Guangping—they were already under UNHCR [UN High Commissioner for Refugees] protection, and the Canadian Government already put them on the resettlement list. Yet, the Chinese Government—under pressure, the government expatriated them and paraded them on TV, so-called confessing their crimes. Now, we do not know where they are being held and they have not been tried for over a year.

Of course, we have all known about the treatment of the Hong Kong—the Causeway Bay bookstore owners. I am so glad that today one of the managers from that bookstore flew from Hong Kong yesterday to come over to tell the stories. He was the only witness, Mr. Hu Zhiwei. He is 75 years' old and the author of 120 books. He witnessed how the bookstore owner, Mr. Lee Bo, was kidnapped by nine mafia-like men, by the Chinese military. They also confiscated over 250,000 copies of the books and secretly transported them back to China and destroyed them into pieces.

The value of monetary loss is over 30 million Hong Kong dollars. I hope our congressional leaders could shake hands with him, encourage him afterward and our media friends can continue to interview him.

He is the only witness, and today is his first time he showed himself with courage. Even in Hong Kong, he was being photographed by the Chinese special agents. When he reported it to the Hong Kong police, that special agent was taken to the police station. An hour later, that agent was released and the Hong Kong police said, "No, we cannot deal with a higher authority from Beijing."

So that is the situation in China today. So thank you very much for your patience.

Chairman SMITH. Pastor Fu, thank you very much.

I just want to point out we have been joined by Ranking Member Walz. Would you like to——

Representative WALZ. No. I will wait.

Chairman SMITH. Okay. Thank you, and thank you for your leadership.

I do want to note that the selection as to the order of the panel is completely arbitrary. This is a panel of extraordinary men and women, heroes, one and all. Again, I want to thank you all for—seven members on a panel is quite large, but you have made the difference and will make a difference going forward.

Our next witness will be Wei Jingsheng. Again, a man who spent 18 years suffering cruelty that is just beyond the pale. And I would like to yield to him.

[The prepared statement of Mr. Fu appears in the appendix.]

STATEMENT OF WEI JINGSHENG, CHAIRMAN, OVERSEAS CHINESE DEMOCRACY COALITION

Mr. WEI. [With the aid of a translator.] I think during the Trump Administration the trade relationship with China will be a major policy he has to force China to improve its human rights conditions, and to increase its open market. I think it will be a very important policy. I think in this regard, CECC could be able to have a very important function.

So to save time, I will let my English be read by my assistant.

When Donald Trump becomes President of the United States, he is planning to abolish the TPP [Trans-Pacific Partnership] and to begin a trade war with China in order to save the U.S. economy. Some people say that this is a disaster. I would say this is the right way that should have started even earlier.

The reality after 16 years well explains my position—granting China permanent most-favored-nation status, that is a permanent normal trade relationship, was a huge mistake. It did not promote the development of the U.S. economy, but was a blood transfusion from the United States to the Chinese economy. It gave China the opportunity to engage in a trade war with the United States.

The reason is as follows. The so-called free trade, refers to a unified law based on the domestic market, thus allowing the free trade. Such a free trade can be carried out normally between countries with a similar legal system. There cannot be normal free trade between countries with completely different legal systems.

For example, after trade with China liberated, there were two main problems: one was cheap labor; one was its uncertain laws that always change.

Since Chinese law does not guarantee human rights, it is able to keep labor prices at a very low level. This has led to the relocation of the U.S. companies to foreign countries, while it also allows Chinese goods to enter the U.S. market with low prices, resulting in unfair competition. It is an important cause of unemployment in the United States.

China's precarious legal system creates serious non-tariff barriers. Any local government can develop their own laws and regulations, without the need to implement the signed treaties and agreements between the Chinese central government and the foreign countries. So they can actually close their targeted import market.

Coupled with the manipulation of the currency by the Chinese central government, those actions increased the exports and created a huge trade surplus for China. This is an important reason causing the economic recession in the United States.

Some people say, for the United States, fighting a trade war with China will end in defeat, at least a lose-lose result. I think such statements are to confuse the U.S. policymakers. I think the United States will win this trade war, while China can only succumb to the rules developed by the United States, otherwise it will accelerate the collapse of the Chinese Communist regime.

My reasons are as follows. First, for the majority of the goods are in the buyers' market. The United States holds the markets, thus it has the power to develop rules, instead of forcing itself to comply with that so-called global free trade rule that cannot be enforced. The United States can formulate its own fair trade rules, to replace the invalid so-called free trade rules.

Second, the Chinese domestic market is narrow and cannot afford the disaster of losing the U.S. market. So China can only compromise on the rules thus to protect part of the market share.

Third, in the past, due to over-expansion of export production of shoddy goods, the quality of Chinese enterprises is very poor. In order to adapt to a fair market in the competition, Chinese companies must quickly upgrade. Therefore, there will be great demand for technology and services from the United States to open up the import market in the United States. This will help expand the U.S. exports and reduce its trade deficit with China.

Fourth, after improving human rights in China, the income of the Chinese working class will increase, therefore the domestic consumer market will expand. This expansion would benefit the U.S. exporters after fair trade, therefore, reducing the U.S. trade deficit and even eliminating it.

So I think that the United States will win the trade war, and in the long run will also be beneficial to the economic normalization in China. China must accept and should accept it.

Thank you.

Chairman SMITH. Mr. Wei, thank you so very much for your leadership and for your testimony today, recommendations.

I would like to now yield to Ms. Rebiya Kadeer.

[The prepared statement of Mr. Wei appears in the appendix.]

STATEMENT OF REBIYA KADEER, PRESIDENT, WORLD UYGHUR CONGRESS

Ms. KADEER. [With the aid of a translator.] Thank you. Chairman Smith and Cochairman Marco Rubio, and respected Members of the Commission, I would like to thank you for holding this timely and important hearing, and thank you for inviting me to testify. I also thank all the people who attended.

So I am trying to learn English so I cannot read my statement. I have prepared a statement. So I would like to ask my assistant to read my written statement.

Since my release from a Chinese prison in 2005, I have reported to the Commission the continuing human rights violations tar-geting the Uyghur people. As the Commission has noted in its an-nual reports, political freedoms in East Turkestan are among the most limited in China. The right to association and assembly is prohibited and freedom of speech is punished severely, as the case of imprisoned Uyghur academic Ilham Tohti illustrates. Economic discrimination, erosion of language rights and religious restrictions add to the already depressing condition of Uyghur human rights.

President Xi Jinping has attempted to codify these violations in a series of repressive laws, such as the ones on counter-terror and cybersecurity. Implementation measures of the counter-terror law at the regional level in East Turkestan are a clear indicator of who China intends to target with these draconian measures.

Nevertheless, China believes it should go further with its suppression. Arbitrary detentions, forced disappearances, and extrajudicial killings continue.

Recent media reports indicate that the Chinese Government has implemented a policy to confiscate passports in East Turkestan to limit the international movement of Uyghurs. This is the formalization of a policy that Uyghur human rights groups have documented since 2006.

Islam is a cornerstone of the Uyghur identity. China has adopted a series of religious laws at the national and regional level that curb Uyghur rights to freedom of worship. Private religious education has been targeted for several years under these measures. However, this year Chinese authorities adopted rules to report parents who encourage their children to undertake religious activities. During the George W. Bush and Barack Obama Administrations my colleagues and I have worked hard to bring Uyghur issues to the attention of the U.S. political community. Our organizations regularly brief State Department officials and legislators at the U.S. Congress. We have managed to mainstream the Uyghur issue into U.S. Government reporting on human rights.

China's heavy-handed policies toward Uyghurs are creating instability and desperation among the Uyghur people. These policies have become self-fulfilling in some respects, as some Uyghurs have become radicalized in their effort to oppose China's oppression.

The United States should be concerned about these developments as it is in the Nation's interest to support the democratic aspirations of the overwhelming majority of the Uyghurs. Stability in East Turkestan, China, and the Central and East Asian regions offers the opportunity to spread American values such as freedom and human rights.

The Administration of President-elect Donald Trump should continue support for the Uyghur struggle for human rights and democracy and step up public concern over rights conditions in East Turkestan with Chinese officials. Any sign that the United States is ready to relinquish its commitment to raising human rights concerns in favor of achieving policy gains elsewhere will be a victory for the Chinese regime.

Furthermore, the incoming administration should exercise extreme skepticism regarding China's narrative that increased militarization and securitization in East Turkestan are justified in fighting radical Islam. The repression that accompanies security measures enables China to keep firm control of the region and suppress legitimate Uyghur claims for greater political, economic, social, and cultural freedoms.

The Trump Administration should understand the situation in East Turkestan in similar terms to Tibet. It is a struggle for cultural survival in the face of formidable assimilative actions by the Chinese state.

Let us be clear. Pressure works. My presence here today is testament to the success of pressuring Chinese officials. My colleagues and I will continue to put forward the Uyghur case to the international community. It is the responsibility of concerned governments to take this case directly to China and urge reform.

The Uyghur people greatly appreciate the United States' support of our plight. However, we ask the incoming administration to publicly raise the Uyghur issue with China.

In conclusion, I offer these recommendations to the Trump Administration:

First, prioritize Uyghur issues, especially during the human rights dialogue and the strategic and economic dialogue with China.

Urge China to allow foreign diplomats and journalists unrestricted access to East Turkestan and Tibet to independently document the conditions in the regions.

Call on China to free Ilham Tohti, Li Xiaobo, and all Uyghur, Chinese, and Tibetan political prisoners.

Ask China to change its repressive policies, which are the root cause of all bloody incidents in the Uyghur region.

Meet Uyghur, Chinese, and Tibetan leaders and human rights activists at the White House.

Create a special coordinator office at the State Department for the Uyghurs.

Finally, ask the Chinese Government to allow my children to leave China.

Thank you.

Chairman SMITH. Thank you so very much, Ms. Kadeer.

I would like to now go to our final witness and thank her for being here. Xiaodan Wang, thank you for speaking out so faithfully on behalf of your dad, especially. The floor is yours. Please?

[The prepared statement of Ms. Kadeer appears in the appendix.]

STATEMENT OF XIAODAN WANG (DANIELLE WANG), FALUN GONG PRACTITIONER AND DAUGHTER OF FORMER POLITICAL PRISONER WANG ZHIWEN

Ms. WANG. Hello everyone. First, I would like to thank the Honorable Representative Smith and Senator Rubio and other honorable Members of the Commission for having me as part of this important hearing.

I am the daughter of Zhiwen Wang, a loving father and kind spirit who has endured the persecution of Falun Dafa since it started on July 20, 1999.

My husband and I returned from China this year empty-handed, shocked, and heartbroken after experiencing the persecution firsthand as U.S. citizens. My story is one of the millions, but I hope it will shed some light on why the U.S. Government's continued role is so critical in ending this atrocity.

In 17 years, there has never been a moment of relief from constant worry about my father's safety. He was arrested and sentenced in December 1999 because he practiced Falun Dafa.

Over the next 15 years, he suffered tremendously; lost his teeth, and had his collar bone broken, and even suffered a stroke in prison one month before his release. Then he was sent to a brainwashing camp in a final attempt to break his spirit in October 2014.

When he made it back home, he was subject to surveillance by police video cameras and neighborhood watch. Even today, he has four agents outside of his front door 24/7.

After my father received his passport in January 2016, my husband and I prepared his immigration and traveled to China in July. This should have been a straightforward trip, but what we encountered was just a small taste of the persecution my father had endured for 17 years.

We were followed by an undercover agent and harassed by police. They tried to intimidate us and get under our skin. They taunted us and abused their power, and ultimately, they slammed the door in our face as we attempted to take the last step to freedom.

We experienced firsthand the discrimination and injustice Falun Dafa practitioners face every day. Regardless of what the Chinese law states, practitioners are treated as criminals, purely for their existence.

The night before our flight home, a group of 30 police and agents showed up in our place in Guangzhou trying to force their way in. They shouted in my face and tried to scare us.

Although they relented eventually, they stationed spies outside of our place to monitor us. We had no choice but to continue on with no one to turn to and no one to protect us.

We left the next morning and drove an hour and a half south of Guangzhou to the city of Dongguan only to be greeted by spies waiting for us at the ferry terminal.

In the end, we could not even make it through Customs. They canceled his passport by cutting it.

To think all of the years of struggle, sleepless nights, and thousands of miles traveled all ended with a pair of scissors is unbelievable. It is still hard for me to bear that I had to leave my father behind in China to face this cruel environment alone. If my father and I did not practice Falun Dafa, I may have broken down completely right there.

I know that not all in China are in support of this persecution. It is the former Chinese Communist Party leader, Jiang Zemin, behind it. Zeng Qinghong, Jiang Zemin's right hand, is also in power in south China and played an important role in denying my father's departure to America.

In addition, the Chinese regime continues its efforts to spread the persecution via propaganda, misinformation, and infiltration.

I ask the new administration, and all officials interacting with their Chinese counterparts to let no opportunity pass by without pushing them on the persecution on Falun Dafa, and the monstrous practice of organ harvesting.

It is crucial that the United States remain true to the role of human rights champion in the world and bring human rights to the center stage in dealing with China.

And finally, I urgently request that the new administration, Department of State, Congress, and all relevant departments help me bring my father home for medical attention so we can finally have our happy ending and a new beginning.

I want to conclude with my dad's thanks. He said, he would like to tell the U.S. Government it actually put his heart at ease when he was in jail because he knew that I was studying in the United States. Thank you.

[The prepared statement of Ms. Wang appears in the appendix.]

Chairman SMITH. Thank you so very much for your testimony. The love of a daughter for her father is just truly inspiring.

Just a couple of things I will mention, ask you a few questions, and yield to my good friend, Mr. Walz.

Pastor Fu, you mentioned the case of Jiang Tianyong who has gone missing. For the record, I would ask unanimous consent that we include this in the record.

Marco Rubio and I sent a letter to the Ambassador of China to the United States on December 7, expressing our deepest concern regarding the recent disappearances of three Chinese citizens, Jiang Tianyong, Liu Feiyue, and Huang Qi and we are hoping for an answer, and we will follow it up with the Embassy to try to get to the bottom of it, and to advocate for them. But, thank you for bringing attention to this.

You did make the point, Pastor Fu, that the human rights situation is the worst in China since the Cultural Revolution. That is the best-kept secret in Washington and in capitals all around the world, as we continue what Chen Guangcheng said in his testimony is an attitude of appeasement toward China that manifests itself all over the United Nations, among nations, and certainly in capitals around the world, including Washington.

So I want to thank you for being bold enough to say exactly— we perhaps, have naive misconceptions about the Chinese dictatorship under Xi Jinping, but as our report this year clearly chronicles, when you look at all of the changes, the new laws, draft laws, and the like that have gone into effect, whether it be on cybersecurity, whether it be on NGOs, and the tightening of the noose around NGOs, which is really a—harbinger of a crackdown, what is happening with regard to religion of all kinds, including the officially recognized churches like the Patriotic or Three Self movement which are being increasingly crushed. The underground is already crushed.

It is time for a significant reappraisal, which you all have helped provide to the Commission, which we will convey to policymakers and also enlighten ourselves.

There are things that could be done immediately by the President-elect when he becomes president. It was not done during President Obama.

On visas, I wrote the law in 2000, The Admiral Nance, Meg Donovan International Foreign Relations Authorization Act of 2000, which is a permanent law that says anybody who was complicit with the barbaric one-child—now, maybe, two-child—per couple policy, but the enforcement mechanisms of coercion remain unabated, can be precluded from issuance of a visa by the United States. It is reason for denial. It has not been implemented in the 16 years that it has been in effect since 2000.

The Global Magnitsky Act is in route to becoming law. It has passed as part of the NDAA [National Defense Authorization Act]. It is in a very good form, I believe. And it can be immediately applicable to Chinese torturers and violators of human rights in our admonition to the administration. When that is signed the next steps would be to start chronicling the names, produce lists of human rights abusers, and then hold them to account. A visa denial is one modest, but meaningful way of doing that. So we will be pushing that, so thank you for raising those issues as well.

Mr. Speaker, you mentioned the worsening of the mistreatment of a Tibetan Buddhist. The New York Times, "China Takes a Chainsaw to a Center of Tibetan Buddhism" by Edward Wong. You are talking about what has gone on in Larung Gar.

You might want to speak to that, because I think that is a highly visible manifestation of the hatred with which the dictatorship holds for faith-filled believers, including Tibetan Buddhists, Uyghurs, Falun Gong, Christians—I mean, it is one thing to profess to be an atheist. You have every right to be an atheist, but you have absolutely no right—and certainly international law is clear on this—to so aggressively suppress, torture, and hurt those who believe in God or in a spiritual practice like Falun Gong.

So you might want to speak to that, if you would. Any of you who would like to speak to the visa ban, and the fact that it should be teed up right now for President Trump to say, we are going to be serious about denying visas to those individuals who commit these atrocities. And also, CPC [Country of Particular Concern]—on religious issues, China has been on the CPC list on a law that was written by former Congressman Frank Wolf, the International Religious Freedom Act of 1998. And Bush did not do much. Obama has done nothing with regard to sanctioning.

As you know, there are prescribed in the International Religious Freedom Act some 18 specific actionable items, the least of which is a demarche, but then there are some very serious ones dealing with trade, security matters, sharing, like cultural exchanges and scientific exchanges that a serious administration could apply to say, "We are not kidding. You have got to let the dissidents go. You have got to end the torture."

We had a hearing in this room recently in which we talked a lot about the torture chair—again, another one of the best-kept secrets in Washington—that is routinely deployed against dissidents to try to break them. So, Mr. Speaker and others, if you want to speak, and then I will yield to Mr. Walz, and then go to Randy Hultgren.

Mr. Tsering. Thank you, Chairman. The ongoing destruction of residences of monks and nuns in Larung Gar is a very serious problem that is facing Tibetan Buddhism today. Larung Gar—some estimate that there are about 20,000 monks and nuns, but nobody has the exact number, but I think it is beyond 10,000 which makes it the largest center of Buddhist learning in the world.

Larung Gar also faced the same fate in the early 2000s, when some part of it was destroyed by the Chinese Government and people started coming back. In fact, if the Chinese Government wanted to destroy it, then why did they allow settlement of monks and nuns in the first place?

So this has resulted in the present problem. Now, the destruction in the case of Larung Gar could be a precursor to many of things that could come, if it is not condemned and stopped, then I am sure the Chinese Government will take this matter to other monasteries. There are already indications that Yargar which is also a monastery linked to Larung Gar may also face the same fate.

In the rest of Tibet, particularly, in the Tibet Autonomous Region, the restrictions of monks and nuns have come down. Those days when Tibet was free and independent, we used to have 7,700 and 5,500, and 3,300 in three big monasteries in Lhasa. Monks and nuns could come from different parts of Tibet to learn in the capital Lhasa, and then go back to their respective regions to teach, preach. They have now brought the numbers down to 500, and still less in those big monasteries.

So Larung Gar is outside of the Autonomous Region, and the learning of Buddhism has increased over the years, not just for Tibetans coming from different parts of Tibet, but also a lot of Han Chinese who have interest in studying Buddhism. In fact, Larung Gar is supposed to have a large number of Han Chinese, and they are also becoming victims of the destruction that is taking place inside Tibet.

This one example can exemplify how the Chinese Government abuses religious freedom inside Tibet. We have been appealing; the Central Tibetan Administration in Dharamsala has released and you must have seen videos of monks and nuns being forced to go back and asked to sing and forced to dance. They were forced to dance and sing praises of the Communist Party after they were sent back to their respective region.

So certain things which are unimaginable are happening, and we hope the U.S. administration will express their concern on the ongoing situation. So we hope the new administration will definitely pay attention to this and bring it to the attention of the Chinese authorities that this is not acceptable to the U.S. Government.

I think the Congress should also adopt resolutions to condemn these kinds of actions by the Chinese Government.

Mr. YANG. I am thrilled. I think that every member of the human rights community is thrilled that the Global Magnitsky Bill actually was passed in the House as part of a National Defense Authorization Act.

We cannot wait to see it signed by the President into law. After that becomes law, we will work closely with CECC and other Congressional organization committees, and the State Department, and the White House.

With the least of these, we think we should ban their travel to the United States. I think this is just the beginning of the paradigm shift as my friend and colleague, Bob Fu, just said—paradigm shift. So I think I have been advocating—this is the second time for me to speak about it at a Congressional hearing—China Democracy Act.

That is the Act that we all stated expressly that advancing human rights in China is in the national interest of this country, and to regulate every Federal agency to promote human rights in China while engaging with China. And also require a presidential report to the Congress about the progress.

The parallel example would be recent because of Taiwan President Tsai Ing-wen's call with President-elect Donald Trump. So Taiwan has been in the headlines, but 37 years back, in Washington, everybody saw the Taiwan situation as inconvenient, just as nowadays. A lot of people present—prime ministers everywhere, see funding human rights issues as inconvenient. So they do not want to do it.

As a policy, we can change—it is very situational. When the situation is not good, they want to change. The major mentality among the policymakers here 37 years ago was to abandon Taiwan altogether because the Taiwan issue had become very inconvenient. But a few Congressional Members insist that we have to defend Taiwan. We have to pass a law to regulate the President of the United States, every one of them have to take the responsibility as a duty of law to defend Taiwan.

So 30-some years passed—then we looked back. This Act actually worked very well for the long-term interest of this country. But at that time, everybody found this inconvenient. This is just as a parallel to the human rights situation here.

The president may find it very inconvenient, but we need the law. We need a China Democracy Act to be passed so that—advancing human rights in China would become a duty of law for every president, and for every Federal agency in this country. Thank you.

Chairman SMITH. Dr. Yang, I would look forward to working with you on that——

Mr. YANG. Yes.

Chairman SMITH (continuing).—legislation. We have talked before. I think your point about U.S. policy failures, we need a different approach. U.S. policy failures need not be forever. It is time to change.

Yes, Mr. Wei?

Mr. WEI. I want to say that the CECC should play an important role in the future trade war with China. During this trade war, human rights and religious rights are a very good reason.

The CECC should really put human rights as a very important target during the future trade war. One side is, it is important to improve human rights. The other side is, to improve human rights would be beneficial to open the Chinese market to U.S. companies.

As a matter of fact, I want to remind you that back 16 years ago when there was a passing of this act about the normal trade relationship, it really has the condition as stipulated, CECC was really in the prospect to determine if this favorable trade relationship is suitable or not when Chinese human rights conditions are really bad.

So we really should remind Donald Trump's team that, yes, the CECC could have used it—to use it for this trade war, but in the meantime, to improve human rights conditions in China. So I think CECC should become a very important tool for this.

Thank you.

Chairman SMITH. Thank you Mr. Wei. Pastor Fu, and then Rebiya Kadeer.

Mr. FU. I want to go further a little bit from what Dr. Yang Jianli just said. We are so happy to see the passage of the Global Magnitsky Act as you have been leading with your colleagues.

I think after this passage we also need to encourage our allies and regional partners to use their influence through the inter-parliamental mechanism to encourage other like-minded parliaments or like a European Parliament to pass a similar measure so that those human rights, religious freedom, rule of law corrupted abusers cannot find any safe sanctuary or haven in any part of the free world.

So we have been working with our partners in Taiwan. I think even the Taiwan Parliament had great momentum with bipartisan, actually tripartisan now, support to make this happen.

Also, I want to illustrate another barring sign about religious freedom. As you know, earlier this year, the Chinese Communist regime made a proposed new regulation on religious affairs. According to this new regulation, those who were fond of so-called illegally organized religious meetings or underground training, like my wife and I did 20 years ago—at that time we received two months' imprisonment, but, according to the newly proposed regulation, if it is passed, those leaders could be subject to up to the equivalent of US$33,000 fine. And of course, point for criminal prosecution, including those who attend overseas religious training or a kind of conference overseas are liable to be punished this way. We just finished a training conference on kind of a biblical—on law and the government on Hong Kong with 400 Christian leaders from mainland China there. This is the first time I found out the Chinese security agents even went to our conference and warned the conference—some of our Hong Kong partners which speakers should be allowed to speak.

The two organizers in Hong Kong were violently beaten up when they returned to China a couple of weeks ago. So you can see the aggressiveness. I think it is a time to have a new paradigm to handle and deal with this kind of worsening situation.

Chairman SMITH. Thank you.

Ms. Kadeer?

Ms. KADEER. So I would like to make a comment about a section in the Uyghur region. It is really very similar to what is happening in Tibet.

There is now new regulations introduced by the Chinese authorities. According to these new regulations, the religious worship outside of the government-designated areas would be considered an illegal religious activity.

So according to Uyghur tradition, according to our religion, we can worship at home. So we can pray at home. According to this new regulation, worshiping at home in private will be considered an illegal religious activity and be punishable by the government. And also now, Chinese authorities encourage the children to re- port about their parents' activities at home. Every week, even elementary school children are being questioned by authorities on what their parents have been doing at home, whether they are worshiping at home.

So there are many families who are destroyed by this, you know, reporting because the children told the school authorities that their parents worshiped at home, so then their parents have been arrested by the Chinese authorities.

And the same thing that happened in Tibet also happened in East Turkestan. The imams of the mosques have been forced to take to the streets and dance and sing praising the Communist Party. Cultural Revolution came back to East Turkestan, so women and men all get forced to take to the streets and sing songs praising their Communist Party and the Chinese Government.

If anybody refuses to take part in these actions, they will be punished or fired from their workplaces. So there are thousands of people who are in Chinese prisons now, suffering in Chinese prisons. All of them have been arrested, detained because of these so-called illegal religious activities.

Thank you.

Chairman SMITH. Chen Guangcheng?

Mr. CHEN. Mr. Chairman, I have two questions. One is before President Obama leaves office, we should press him to call Mr. Xi Jinping about the whereabouts of the attorney, lawyers that disappeared.

And from the performance of the president during his eight years in office, we see that he never met any democracy activists, and dissidents from China. But actually, he spared his very valuable time to meet with Jack Ma, the billionaire of the Chinese.

I wonder why the president has forgotten his duty to preserve the founding principle of the United States as a human rights protector and defender? And I hope that the new Trump Administration will adopt an agenda to end authoritarian regime with the help of the Chinese people there.

I think that before Chinese human rights improve, I do not think America has any other choices.

Thank you.

Chairman SMITH. Mr. Chen, on that question—it was part rhetorical, but I think it deserves at least some focus.

In not meeting with the dissidents, and we have asked the President to meet both in Beijing when he travels there, and in the White House with dissidents—when Bush went to the Olympics, we asked him to meet with dissidents like Rebiya Kadeer and others, and he did. Wei, you will remember that. And he spent a considerable amount of time before setting foot into Beijing getting insights from the people who had suffered.

The one that has troubled me the most is that after we had our Five Daughters hearing—we had five precious daughters of dissidents who are, today, still languishing in prison, including the daughter of Gao Zhisheng, who appealed to the President. Each of the five said, "Mr. President, you have two daughters. You will understand. We want to meet with you and ask that you raise our father's cases by name with the President of China."

We sent over that request. They made it themselves. The Washington Post did an outstanding article on it, by the editorial page editor. It was December 2013, on the House Foreign Affairs subcommittee hearing, the Five Daughters hearing. We called repeatedly down to the White House. Will you meet, please, Mr. President with the five daughters who are young ladies?

One wrote a beautiful piano song. She is a great pianist, but she wrote a song to her dad, and she just wanted to look the President in the eye and say, "Please advocate for our dads' release, to the end of the torture."

After six months, we got back from the White House, he does not have the time.

Mr. CHEN. I would like to add one more thing.

As we mentioned Mr. Jiang Tianyong, disappearing attorney, it was him who showed up at 2 a.m., at the wee hours in Beijing, during the President's visit because they learned that the President's office released a statement and said, "Oh, no human rights advocates showed up during his visit." But that was not the case. So I want to emphasize that too.

Chairman SMITH. I would just add, Danielle was one of those five daughters. And, again, all we wanted was a face-to-face meeting so that the President could hear their appeals.

I yield to my good friend.

Representative WALZ. Yes. Thank you to the Chairman.

I would suggest, then, we put in a formal request to President-elect Trump to make that meeting from us as Commissioners. I would certainly be glad to sign that because I think it is what we ask for.

I think maybe Yang Jianli brought up the idea of inconvenience. I think sometimes the Chinese Government feels like we will—we are not persistent, or we will lose our focus, or things that are inconvenient we will put aside.

I would suggest to them that they have not met Chairman Smith, because he will not give up. He will be persistent, and I think that is what we need. So I think that is exactly what we should do.

To each of you, it is a privilege to be here with you, and every time I come, I am inspired, I am encouraged, and I realize that the fight goes on. At times thinking, as a Member of Congress, what can I do? Then I watch extraordinary people in circumstances sometimes beyond imagination rise up on those very issues that are our core foundation issues of human rights, and that is truly inspiring.

It is from these hearings, and it is from each of you who have testified before—some of us have become friends over the years—that told us you need to continue to talk. I think we have spoken on this, and to let some of you know last year we traveled to Hong Kong, to Tibet, and then met with Premier Li in the Forbidden City.

I can assure each of you it was something I thought I would never witness. Sitting in the Forbidden City with the Premier of China and him answering questions about His Holiness the Dalai Lama, him asking questions and answering questions about Falun Gong, about the Uyghurs, about freedom of religion, in Hong Kong. And I can tell you this, that Ambassador Baucus along with Leader Pelosi, myself, and other Members of Congress did meet with those dissidents in Beijing in the U.S. Embassy, and it is a good thing we have divided government because we have a voice. We continue to speak out on these issues, we continue to find common ground. So I cannot tell you the courage you give me, the instruction that you give me to continue talking because many of us up here worry the inconvenience, or more importantly, it is one thing for us to say what we are going say, and then go to our homes while your families are still in Chinese prisons, while your families are still under threat, the feedback we have gotten from you is, continue to make this issue.

I will just ask, or maybe make a statement, maybe rhetorical a little bit. Wei Jingsheng brought up this point about tying trade to human rights. Those of us in here know going back to President Clinton, most-favored-nation status and some of the changes—I certainly was under the illusion that liberalizing trade and openness would have a significant impact on liberalization of personal freedoms.

I have now seen that is not the case. As I told someone—again, it is anecdotal, but I can tell you this. I have been to Hong Kong dozens, and dozens, and dozens of times, both going from Fosan as a young teacher to Hong Kong, and coming here.

The last time I went—and certainly it was the first time as a U.S. Congressman, Hong Kong is significantly different. Hong Kong feels different, and it feels different in one of those most basic ways of personal freedoms, religious freedoms, freedom of expression. And those should be concerns of ours.

I think going—I would say this, just as a suggestion, I am not sure President-elect Trump would characterize it as a trade war, but I do think he should probably characterize it as a recalibration of fair trade. I think as a Nation, this is an important discussion we should have.

We may get cheaper products at our local big box store, but it comes at a price. It comes at a price as workers as Wei Jingsheng said. It comes at a price in wages. It comes at a price in our economy, but it also comes at a price to human rights for those workers. It comes at a price that we have lost our leverage.

I would say this. I am very encouraged that it appears that incoming Defense Secretary, General Mattis has impressed upon President-elect Trump that torture is not something that we do, and it is not something that we accept from others.

I think this does give us a chance to reset. This does give us an opportunity because of a peaceful transitioning government here to highlight those things, and I would say that each of you said this, I think this Commission can be a place for that to start again.

I think you have got a Chairman that has been dogged about it. You have got a Chairman that has been consistent across administrations. When they fail or fall short, he has called them out. When they have done something right or leading in that right direction, he has praised them for that.

I think I do not speak for all of the Commissioners, but I agree with that. I, for one, am serious. I think we send a letter and ask the President-elect to meet with the five daughters if that is what we are going to ask.

We should be prepared that that may not happen, too. I think as a Commission, it may or it may not, but our responsibility is clear and it comes from each of you saying this. We need to continue to press these issues. We need to continue to recalibrate how we do this.

I think we underestimate the leverage of both—by our actions— this was a fascinating thing, and I never thought this would happen. Premier Li was really fascinating because I told them I had been to Tibet before. And I said I had been to Tibet in 1989. And they said, "No, it was February of 1990." They are very good at remembering when I was there, better than I. [Laughter.]

They said, "Has it not improved?" And I said, "Well, it was easier than going by bus for seven days from Chengdu, because now we could fly in or take the train. There were more hospitals. There were more shops." But I told them candidly, speaking face-to-face, I said it is very different. The culture is very different.

And he said, well, you saw a village or whatever. Yes, a Potemkin village that they showed us that was not there.

But he brought up something very interesting that showed me that this relationship is changing a little bit. He said, "Congressman, I know when you were a young man, you taught on the Pine Ridge Native American Reservation in South Dakota. How did America treat the Native Americans?"

And I answered to him, "I would not use us as an example of the right way to do it because many of us know there are things we could do differently. We are asking you in the spirit of friendship, cooperation, human rights to work with these issues and to understand all of us have to go through that."

And it was fascinating to me that the Premier was gracious, he engaged in this conversation. I did not have any expectations there would be a change, but I think it did show if we continue to bring these issues up, if we continue to lead with our values, and tie those to our economic policies, not separate them from that, that there is potential here for us to get to a common ground.

I think for all of us, we have to continue to believe that because whether it is our father, whether it is our relatives, whether it is our own family being asked to make gripping choices, we have to see a better day.

So again, I thank each of you. I do not have a question of you, but I think it is important to stress the inspiration you bring to others, the courage that you bring to others, and to speak about an issue from the United States, I know does not take courage. To stand up and say it in Beijing or in Foshan, or in Guangdong, those take courage understanding there will be repercussions. This issue of basic human rights, it unites all of us.

So I thank the Chairman once again for putting together a remarkable panel. I do think it needs to be said, your persistence on the issue of human rights is something incredibly admirable. It is something that every day I am glad you are still here, because I do think—and the Chinese know this—they just want to wear you down over time. They want to wear you down. I have seen it. They found the one person they are not going to wear down. So I am glad to be with him.

I yield back.

Chairman SMITH. Thank you very much. I thank you for your leadership for decades on behalf of human rights in China, and I think the idea that you suggested is a great one. We will follow it up, and it will be a letter from you and I, and, of course, the other—the Cochair and I am sure Marco will readily agree with that.

Is there anything else anybody would like to say before we conclude? [No response.]

For the record, I would ask unanimous consent that statements from the 709 Lawyers' Wives and the Southern Mongolian Human Rights Information Center be made a part of the record. Without objection, so ordered.

Again, thank you all for your insights. This is a new beginning. The failed policies by any previous administration need to be matriculated to something that works. You have given us the blueprint.

Thank you so very much. The hearing is adjourned.

[The statements appear in the appendix.]

[Whereupon the hearing was concluded at 4:08 p.m.]

APPENDIX

PREPARED STATEMENTS

PREPARED STATEMENT OF PENPA TSERING

DECEMBER 7, 2016

Thank you for this opportunity to testify before the Congressional-Executive Commission on China regarding on our recommendations to the next United States Congress and Administration on human rights in Tibet. This is my first testimony before the United States Congress following my appointment as Representative of H.H. the Dalai Lama to the Americas. Therefore, I would like to begin with offering the gratitude of the Tibetan people to the United States Congress for your consistent and strong support to His Holiness the Dalai Lama and the Tibetan issue.

Through its elections the United States and the American people have shown democracy in practice. Following the results, His Holiness the Dalai Lama has written to both President-Elect Donald Trump and Secretary Hillary Clinton. His Holiness further looks forward to meeting with the new President, just as he has done with the previous several presidents.

At the outset, for those who don't much about Tibet, I wish to present few basic facts. Some people feel that Tibet is a very small country nestled in the Himalayas. Factually, Tibet with close to 6 million Tibetans live on 2.14 Million Sq. Kms, roughly 23 percent of China's total landmass. Tibet has an average altitude of 4641 meters or 15226 feet above sea level. Tibetans call Tibet as the Land surrounded by snow mountains; westerners called Tibet as the roof of the world; Asians call Tibet as the water tower of Asia and today Chinese environmental scientists call Tibet as the third pole because of the amount of glaciers and permafrost that feeds all the major rivers of Asia.

ISSUES

On the matter of our recommendations, while there has been a clear deterioration in the overall human rights situation in Tibet, I would like to raise the following four points that can have grave impact during the term of the next Congress and Administration.

1. Religious freedom of the Tibetan people

Several developments in recent times, which follow decades of oppressive policies, indicate that in order to fulfil their political agenda, the Chinese authorities are undermining the very existence of a genuine Tibetan Buddhist tradition in Tibet.

These include adopting regulations that give the Chinese Communist Party the absolute decision making authority on matters concerning Tibetan Buddhism, including promulgating legislation requiring all reincarnated Tibetan Buddhist leaders to obtain government approval. These measures are aimed at controlling and managing the process of the Dalai Lama's next reincarnation, in order to ensure the dominance of the Party state in Tibet. Chinese official media reports have confirmed that the CCP authorities view the matter of the Dalai Lama's reincarnation as "an important issue concerning sovereignty and national security." What the Chinese government has done to the Panchen Lama, who was kidnapped when he was 5 years old and has no longer been seen since then and replaced him with someone appointed by the Chinese Communist Party, is a stark reminder of what China intends to do.

Secondly, there has been increased and intrusive interference in the affairs of the Tibetan Buddhist monasteries and institutes. The most recent case is the demolition process taking place at the Tibetan Buddhist Academy of Larung Gar in Tibet—one of the world's largest monastic institutions with a population of thousands of Chinese and Tibetan practitioners - and the forced expulsion of several hundreds of monks and nuns from there. Larung Gar has in recent years become a vital center for the study, practice, and promotion of Buddhist teachings.

The most recent demolitions of monks' and nuns' dwellings began in July due to restrictions put in place by the Chinese government. According to information received from Tibet, hundreds of monks and nuns from Golog (Chinese: Guoluo) and Jyegudo (Chinese: Yushu) in Qinghai, Ngaba (Chinese: Aba) in Sichuan, and the Tibet Autonomous Region were among those forced to leave Larung Gar in late October this year. Officials and police arrived from their home areas to escort them. Many monks and nuns were compelled to put their thumbprints or sign a document which stated the following in Chinese: In accordance with the requirements of promoting regulation work in the Serthar County Larung Five Sciences Buddhist Academy, I left the Larung Five Sciences Buddhist Academy and will, after returning home, as always continue to love the country and love religion, and abide by the law. I solemnly promise not to return to the Serthar County Larung Five Sciences Buddhist Academy, except to carry out relevant formalities during large-scale Buddhist activities."

If we do not send a strong message to the Chinese authorities on this, it could be a precursor to many such demolitions of other Tibetan religious institutes.

2. Restrictions of Freedom of Movement

From 2012, following the imposition of tough new measures restricting travel in Tibetan areas since the 2008 protests, Tibetans began to face tightening restrictions on their travel abroad, through restrictions on the issuance of passports, including to receive Buddhist teachings from the Dalai Lama, or to study abroad. This is in contrast to the increasing number of Chinese citizens being granted passports and being able to travel abroad with ease.

Since the Dalai Lama is giving an important Tibetan Buddhist teaching in India in January 2017, many Tibetans in Tibet wanted to travel there. In addition to the already existing restrictions for Tibetans in getting a passport, in the last few weeks, Chinese officials have confiscated passports from those Tibetans who have managed to secure one.

Some Tibetans who have already arrived in Nepal and India for pilgrimage and for attending the Buddhist teachings in January have already been ordered to return, and the authorities are as well pressuring their families in Tibet.

China's discriminatory policy on Tibetan freedom of movement also includes Tibetan Americans who wish to travel to Tibet for pilgrimage or to meet their relatives. The Chinese Embassy and consulates in the United States adopt a different processing system for Tibetan Americans that includes intensive investigation and often end up with denial of visas.

3. Use of Counter-terrorism measures to control Tibetans

In Tibet, despite the absence of any violent insurgency, an aggressive "counter-terrorism" drive has been underway resulting in the militarization across the Tibetan plateau. By conflating the expression of distinct religious and ethnic identities with "separatism", and blurring distinctions between violent acts and peaceful dissent, the Chinese government is using counter-terrorism as a justification to crackdown on even mild expressions of religious identity and culture in Tibet.

In line with a "counter-terror" campaign, the Chinese authorities have rolled out new systematic and long-term security measures in Tibet as part of an intensified control agenda.

While rigorous and oppressive measures, including an increase in Communist Party personnel at "grass roots" levels, have been in place since the 2008 protests in the Tibet Autonomous Region (TAR), these measures to eliminate dissent and enforce compliance to Chinese Communist Party policies are now being increasingly observed in the eastern Tibetan areas of Kham and Amdo.

Since October 2011, Chinese authorities have sent tens of thousands of government and party cadres to thousands of villages, religious institutions and neighborhood to monitor and surveil local Tibetans, organize anti-Dalai Lama themed political indoctrination campaigns, and entrench and expand the influence of the CCP in Tibet.

4. H.H. the Dalai Lama and the Tibetan issue

On the overall issue of Tibet, the position of His Holiness the Dalai Lama remains unchanged in key areas. His is commitment to the Middle Way is unwavering. He is not seeking independence for Tibet but, rather, genuine, meaningful autonomy for the Tibetan people within the People's Republic of China reached through a negotiated settlement with the Chinese leadership. He has strengthened democratic values within the Tibetan community in exile, including in handing over all his political authority to the elected Tibetan leadership.

Diplomatic and Political Actions that have worked:

1. Presidential meeting with His Holiness the Dalai Lama

Successive Presidents of United States have met with His Holiness the Dalai Lama and expressed their support for the Middle Way Approach. This sends a very strong signal to the Chinese authorities that the Issue of Tibet is on the highest of agenda in US-China relations.

2. Appointment and the role of Special Coordinator on Tibet

Having a special coordinator on Tibetan Issues in the State Department as mandated by the US Tibet Policy Act of 2002 and its annual report on the status of Sino-Tibet negotiations indicates the importance that US Administration attaches in resolving the Tibetan issue in a non-violent, mutually beneficial negotiated solution without pre-conditions.

3. Hearings and reports of the commissions

Meetings of His Holiness the Dalai Lama, Sikyong, and the Speaker of the Tibetan Parliament in Exile with bipartisan, bicameral congressional Foreign Relations Committee; hearings and reports by CECC and Tom Lantos Human Rights Commission helps in informing the congress of the Tibetan perspective of the situation inside Tibet and possible solutions.

4. Financial Aids

Financial Aids from State Departments to the Tibetans through USAID, PRM and Scholarship Programs for education, health, social and economic development of Tibetans helps in the preservation and promotion of Tibetan identity.

5. Bills and Resolutions

We believe that the introduction of the Reciprocal Access to Tibet bill has built some traction in allowing congressional delegation and journalists visits to Tibet.

6. Congressional and State Department visits to Tibet and Dharamsala

The congressional delegation's visit to China and Tibet provided first hand understanding of the situation inside Tibet and more intimate dialogue with the local leaders. Similarly, visits to Dharamsala also sends a strong signal to China.

Suggestions to the new Administration and the Congress:

1. The United States has played a pivotal role in highlighting the human rights situation in Tibet and in encouraging the Chinese Government to improve them. Human rights will be respected if China implements internal reform. US Government need to publicly express concern for the human rights situation in Tibet to send a clear signal to China that this is an integral part of US policy on China

2. Advocate for the release of Tibetan political prisoners. The US should advocate for the release of specific Tibetan political prisoners languishing in Chinese prisons. In the past, efforts by the United States and other governments have led to the Chinese authorities releasing some Tibetan political prisoners who were able to come to the United States for medical treatment and rehabilitation. My office will be pleased to provide some names of Tibetan political prisoners.

3. An early implementation of the Tibetan Policy Act, including the designation of the US Special Coordinator for Tibetan Issues at a senior level within the State Department so that the new Administration has its contact person on Tibet in place for effective coordination of work.

4. The Reciprocal Access to Tibet Act before the House could also help to promote access to Tibetan areas for U.S. officials, journalists, and citizens. Currently, travel restrictions imposed by the Chinese government on Tibet are more severe than for any other provincial-level entity in China. The approval of the Global Magnitsky Act by the US Congress will send the right message to Chinese officials responsible for human rights violations in Tibet.

5. The Administration should impress on China the need to establish US Consulate in Lhasa.

6. The incoming President should meet with His Holiness the Dalai Lama at the earliest opportunity in keeping with precedents.

7. The congress and the Administration could raise with the Chinese leadership their discriminatory policies towards the Tibetan people, particularly in the matters of religious freedom and freedom of movement.

8. The Administration should monitor China's misuse of counter terrorism policies in Tibet leading to the denial of fundamental rights of the Tibetan people. As and when necessary this needs to be raised publicly.

9. Preserve funding for Tibet-related programs in the Department of State & Foreign Operations Appropriations bill, including economic development; humanitarian assistance; Tibetan language broadcasts through Voice of America and Radio Free Asia; and scholarship and exchange programs. These small but indispensable investments in Tibetan communities support the Dalai Lama's vision of preserving Tibetan identity during these difficult times until a negotiated agreement is reached.

10. The congress should organize more bipartisan, bicameral visits to Tibet and Dharamsala.

11. Above all, proactive support at the highest level of Government to encourage the Chinese authorities to resume dialogue to resolve the Tibetan issue, as mandated by the Tibetan Policy Act, will eventually improve the human rights situation of the Tibetan people.

I thank you for the opportunity to testify before your Commission and look forward to answering any questions you have.

Priority list: Tibetan Political Prisoners at Risk
International Campaign for Tibet - October 2016

Druklo (Shokjang)

Name: Druklo (pen-name Shokjang)
Chinese: 雪江
Status: Sentenced to 3 years in February 2016

Druklo, more widely known by his pen name Shokjang, is known for his reflective and thought-provoking articles on issues of contemporary concern such as ethnic policy and settlement of nomads. There was widespread dismay when he was detained by security police in Rebkong (Chinese: Tongren) on March 19 2015, with numerous netizens expressing their sadness. On 17 February 2016, he was sentenced to three years in prison in a court in Xining, the provincial capital of Qinghai. Details of charges are not known, although one source in exile said that he believed it was connected to 'separatism'. In the days leading up to his arrest, Druklo wrote a blog post about an intense build up of Chinese security forces in the Rebkong area.

More information at:
https://www.savetibet.org/popular-courageous-tibetan-blogger-sentenced-to-three-years-in-prison/
http://www.savetibet.org/popular-tibetan-blogger-asserts-his-innocence-in-letter-from-prison/

Tashi Wangchuk

Name: Tashi Wangchuk
Chinese: 扎西旺秀
Status: Detained since January 2016

Tashi Wangchuk, 31, has been detained by police in his home area of Jyegudo (Chinese: Yushu) in Qinghai since 27 January 2016, following an interview with the New York Times on Tibetan culture and language, published as an article and video in November 2015 (the video is available at:http://www.nytimes.com/2015/11/29/world/asia/china-tibet-language-education.html?_r=1). He faces charges of 'separatism', although he has not advocated Tibetan independence, and has said that Tibet should have greater regional autonomy, especially in the issue of language, under Chinese governance. According to information from the lawyer cited by the New York Times, the police concluded an additional investigation at the prosecutors' request on 25 August 2016, and handed over those results. Prosecutors must now decide whether the case should go to court. Tashi Wangchuk is being held at the main detention center in Yushu (in the Tibetan area of Kham), where he lives with his elderly parents.

More information at: https://www.savetibet.org/imprisoned-tibetan-language-advocate-tashi-wangchuk-faces-false-separatism-charges/

Thamkey Gyatso

Name: Thamkey Gyatso
Chinese: 坦科加错 (Tan-Ke-JiaCuo)
Status: Sentenced to 15 years in

Tibetan Buddhist monk Thamkey Gyatso, from Labrang Tashikyil monastery, is serving a 15-year sentence following his involvement in peaceful political protests in 2008 and possibly also linked to his writings for literary journals. Thamkey Gyatso, who is in his early thirties, was arrested on April 29, 2008 in Labrang, following the major protests in March, 2008. Although he was known to be in good health before his detention, the right side of Thamkey's body is now paralyzed and he can no longer walk. *"His right eye, ear, hand and leg are no longer functional,"* said a Tibetan source. *"He has received some medical treatment but nothing that has helped him to recover. He is unable to move and he just sits on a wheelchair. He can still speak slowly and recognize people."*

Lobsang Kunchok and Lobsang Tsering

Name: Lobsang Kunchok
Chinese: 洛桑贡觉
Sentence: Sentenced to life in January 2013

In January 2013, a Tibetan monk named Lobsang Kunchok was given a death sentence suspended for two years (normally converted to life), and his nephew Lobsang Tsering sentenced to ten years for "intentional homicide" connected to the self-immolation of eight Tibetans in Ngaba (Chinese: Aba) - although five of the self-immolations never occurred. The two Tibetans were caught up in a new drive by Chinese authorities to criminalize the self-immolations in Tibet, and the severe sentences were the first to be imposed against individuals who have allegedly 'incited' or 'coerced' Tibetans to self-immolate. The sentences were handed down by the Intermediate People's Court of the Ngaba Tibetan and Qiang Autonomous Prefecture. On January 28, Xinhua had acknowledged that the two Tibetans were not represented by their own lawyers. Despite an assertion by a judge who told the Global Times that: *"authorities obtained sufficient evidence showing it [the alleged crimes] had been instructed by 'forces from abroad',"* no evidence was presented to justify the sentencing.

Konchok Tsephel

Name in Tibetan (Wylie): Dkon mchog tshe 'phel
Chinese: 贡觉次白, 贡却才培
Status: Sentenced to 15 years in November 2009

Konchok Tsephel, born in 1970, in Machu (Ch: Maqu), Gannan TAP, Gansu province. He was an official in a Chinese government environmental department and founder of the influential Tibetan literary website, *Chodme* ('Butter-Lamp', www.tibetcm.com), detained on February 26, 2009 and sentenced in November 2009 to 15 years of imprisonment after a closed-door trial at the Intermediate People's Court of Kanlho (Chinese: Gannan) Tibetan Autonomous Prefecture, Gansu province. From February to early November 2009, his family had no idea where he was. He was sentenced "on charges of disclosing state secrets," according to reports from Tibet received by Tibetan exiles. Some of the charges are believed to relate to content on his website, which aims to protect Tibetan culture, and passing on information about last year's protests in Tibet.

Topden

Name: Topden
Chinese: 刀登
Status: Sentenced to 5 years

Topden, a 30-year old nomad and writer who writes under the pseudonym Dro Ghang Gah, was sentenced to five years in prison for "keeping contacts with Dalai clique and for engaging in activities to split the nation". He was detained following unrest in the Driru region in Nagchu. Tibetan sources believe that his imprisonment was to punish him for writing a poem detailing the suffering of Tibetans in the county. The poem gives details of the crackdown including the incommunicado detention of a 69-year old layman, mining at a local sacred mountain, and the early years of Chinese rule in the late 1960s when thousands of Tibetans were starved, imprisoned and killed.

Wangdu

Name in Tibetan (Wylie): Dbang'dus
Chinese: 旺堆
Status: Sentenced to life in December 2008

Wangdu, who worked for an international public health NGO, was sentenced in December 2008 to life imprisonment after he allegedly shared information about the situation in Tibet. Wangdu, a former Project Officer for an HIV/AIDS program in Lhasa run by the Australian Burnet Institute, was charged with 'espionage' by the Lhasa City Intermediate People's Court after he was detained on

March 14, 2008, the day that demonstrations turned violent in Lhasa. Wangdu was accused of collecting *"intelligence concerning the security and interests of the state and provid[ing] it to the Dalai clique...prior to and following the 'March 14' incident"*.

Migmar Dhondup

Name in Tibetan (Wylie): Mima Dunzhu
Chinese: 米玛顿珠
Status: Sentenced to 14 years

Migmar Dhondup, who was also arrested in connection with the March 14 (2008) protests and has been sentenced to 14 years imprisonment, is in his early thirties and also worked for an NGO doing community development work. He is originally from Tingri (Chinese: Dingri), in Shigatse (Chinese: Xigaze), Tibet Autonomous Region. Migmar Dhondup, who speaks fluent English and is very well educated, also used to work as a tour guide. Like Wangdu, he was accused of collecting "intelligence concerning the security and interests of the state and provid[ing] it to the Dalai clique...prior to and following the 'March 14' incident.

Yeshe Choedron

Name: Yeshe Choedron
Chinese: 益西曲珍
Status: Sentenced to 15 years in November 2008

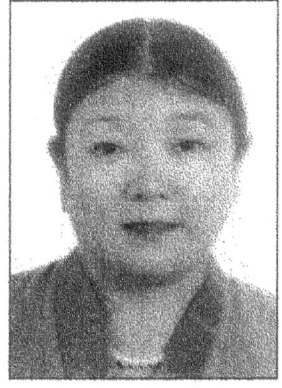

Yeshe Choedron was arrested in March 2008. On November 7, 2008, the Lhasa Intermediate People's Court sentenced Yeshe Choedron to 15 years imprisonment after being convicted for "espionage" for allegedly providing "intelligence and information harmful to the security and interests of the state" to "the Dalai clique's security department," according to the Lhasa Evening News (an official party newspaper). She was 53 years old at the time of her arrest. In 2016, Yeshe Choedron was awarded the inaugural 'Tenzin Delek Rinpoche Medal of Courage' a new international Tibetan human rights defenders award created in memory of the late popular monk Trulku Tenzin Delek Rinpoche, who died in Chinese prison in July 2015.

Gartse Jigme

Name in Tibetan (Wylie):
Chinese: 嘎孜久买
Status: Sentenced to 5 years in 2013

A respected Tibetan monk, Jigme Gyatso (also known as Gartse Jigme based on the name of his monastery in Amdo) was sentenced to five years in prison on January 3, 2013, after writing two books on the situation in Tibet and the suffering of Tibetan people. Gartse Jigme's third book, which was seized by police from the publishers' before printing, includes a discussion on the self-immolations in Tibet and Chinese policy. The sentencing of Gartse Jigme followed the screening of a new Chinese state media documentary seeking to blame exile Tibetans for the self-immolations in Tibet since 2009 (http://www.savetibet.org/resource-center/maps-data-fact-sheets/self-immolation-fact-sheet).The new propaganda video is part of a more aggressive and formalized drive against the self-immolations that has involved the imposition of long prison sentences to Tibetans accused of 'inciting' these actions. Gartse Jigme Gyatso was detained by police in his room at Gartse monastery in Tsekhog (Chinese: Zeke Xian) county in Malho (Chinese: Huangnan) Tibetan Autonomous Prefecture), Qinghai on January 3 (2013) and taken to Xining.

OTHER CASES OF CONCERN

Gedhun Choekyi Nyima (11th Panchen Lama)

Name: Gedhun Choekyi Nyima
Chinese: 更登确吉尼玛
Status: Detained since May 1995 – Whereabouts unknown

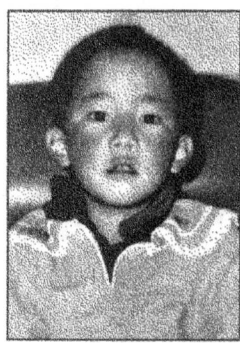

Gedhun Choekyi Nima was just six years old when he was recognized by His Holiness the Dalai Lama as the 11th Panchen Lama, one of Tibet's most important religious leaders. Shortly after, on 17 May 1995, he and his family were taken into custody by the Chinese authorities. While they have admitted taking him, they have continually refused to divulge any information about him or his whereabouts, making his case an enforced disappearance.

Dhondup Wangchen

Chinese: 顿珠旺钦 also 当知项欠
Status: Sentenced to 6 years, released, request family reunion by allowing him out of Tibet

Dhondup Wangchen was detained in March 2008, soon after he completed filming a documentary

("Leaving Fear Behind") featuring Tibetans in a Tibetan area of Qinghai expressing their views on the Dalai Lama, the Olympic Games, and Chinese laws. Police detained filmmaker him on March 26, 2008 in Kawasumdo (Chinese: Tongde) county, Tsolho (Chinese: Hainan) TAP, Qinghai province, and his assistant Jigme Gyatso, a Labrang (Chinese: Xiahe) Tashikhyil monk, on March 23 (Jigme Gyatso later escaped from prison to India, and is now living in Switzerland). The men filmed more than 100 Tibetans, most of whom chose to speak on camera without concealing their identities. The film was smuggled out of China prior to the film-makers' detention. The documentary, featuring 20 of the Tibetans, was screened in August 2008. Police held Dhondup Wangchen for 3 months at Ershilipu detention center, near Xining city, and then in a hotel. He is believed to be still in Ershilipu, but there is currently no news on them.

The film "Leaving Fear Behind" can be viewed in its entirety (around 25 minutes) at *http://woeser.middle-way.net/2008/09/leaving-fear-behind.html*

ICT United States	**ICT Europe**	**ICT Germany**	**ICT Belgium**
1825 Jefferson Place, NW	Vijzelstraat 77	Schönhauser Allee 163	11, rue de la linière
Washington, DC 20036	1017HG Amsterdam	10435 Berlin	1060 Brussels
United States of America	The Netherlands	Germany	Belgium
Phone: +(1) 202-785-1515	Phone: +31 (0)20 3308265	Telefon: +49 (0)30 27879086	Phone: +32 (0)2 609 44 10
Fax: (202) 785-434	Fax: +31 (0)20 3308266	Fax: +49 (0)30 27879087	Fax: +32 (0)2 609 44 32
info@savetibet.org	icteurope@savetibet.nl	info@savetibet.de	info@savetibet.eu
www.savetibet.org	www.savetibet.nl	www.savetibet.de	www.savetibet.fr

Statement Submitted by **Dr. YANG Jianli***

To the Congressional-Executive Commission on China (CECC) hearing titled, "Dissidents Who Have Suffered for Human Rights in China: A Look Back and A Look Forward", Dec.7, 2016.

Contents:

A.

Democracy for China: Missed Opportunities and Opportunities Ahead

The 1989 pro-democracy movement stood against government corruption and for democracy and freedom. This movement was widespread but ended in bloodshed. The Tiananmen massacre created a strong sense of fear and dismay of general politics among ordinary people. Any room for a public system of checks and balances against governmental abuse of power was taken away.

It also created a sense of fear and crisis within the Communist regime, because it had brought unprecedented public awareness to human rights and democracy. Life was no longer the same for the rulers who had to face a completely different domestic and international environment.

The subsequent disintegration of the Soviet Union and the Eastern European Bloc cast an even heavier cloud over the heads of Chinese Communist officials. "How long can the red flag continue to fly?" They all started to doubt.

To be sure, the CCP regime was struggling to survive the Tiananmen crisis, for which breaking international isolation was one of the imperatives facing the regime. Less than three weeks after the Massacre when China's leadership was least assertive and most susceptible to outside pressures, President Bush secretly sent his special envoy National Security Adviser Brent Scowcroft to meet with Deng Xiaoping and other Chinese leaders.

The meeting, later made public, did not seem to bring about any tangible results for either side. But this very gesture of President Bush's reveled America's weakness and assured China's leadership the US's intention to continue the recognition of, and maintain the normal relations with, the repressive regime even if there was no indication of its willingness to admit or correct its serious mistakes or crimes. On July 28, 3 weeks after his special envoy returned to Washington, President Bush wrote a second, extremely carefully worded letter to Deng Xiaoping. "Please understand", wrote Bush, "that this letter has been personally written, and is coming from one who wants to go forward together. Please don't be angry with me if I have crossed the invisible threshold laying between constructive suggestion and 'internal interference'..." What could that imply? Judge for yourselves.

Democrats, especially Governor Bill Clinton in his campaign trail, harshly criticized Bush for "kowtowing" to China, while some conservatives saw Bush's move in the aftermath of the Tiananmen incident as premature in the absence of conciliatory gestures from Beijing. Different China views were reflected in the debate on whether and how to continue to grant China a MFN trade status.

One side of the debate, led by Rep. Nancy Pelosi and Senator George Mitchell, asserted that US trade relations with

China must be linked to China's human rights record. We, Chinese democracy activists, supported this idea because we understood that without such a linkage, continuing normal trade with China would be like a blood transfusion to the CCP regime, making it more aggressive and harming the interests of both the American and Chinese people. This idea was embodied in Pelosi and Mitchell's legislation in 1993. But one year after assuming presidency, President Clinton took a 180 degree turn and reversed the policy. The reversal was based on the theory, which was widely upheld by corporations, columnists pundits and policy makers, that trade would lead to democracy because trade would inevitably result in economic growth and the growth of the middle class which would in turn demand more political freedom.

This theory does not seem to apply to China, at least up to this point.

With money and technology pouring in from the U.S. and other Western countries, the Chinese Communist regime not only survived the 1989 crisis, it catapulted into the 21st century. The country's explosive economic growth lifted it from one of the poorest countries to become the number two economy in the world; but China remains firmly near the bottom of indicators on democratic development. Over the years China's middle class have largely been acquiescent to its one-party dictatorship and its gross violations of human rights. What has gone wrong, in China and the international community?

Let's look at China.

In 1992, when the Americans were heatedly debating about China policy and about to delink human rights from trade, Deng Xiaoping took the famous Southern Inspection Tour to further economic opening up. Communist officials at all levels soon realized three realities: First, the Chinese Communist Party's stay in power has nothing to do with communist ideals. Second, "economic growth means everything;" that is, continued economic growth is the last, best hope to keep the CCP ship afloat. Third, in order to uphold the one-party dictatorship, it had to rely on capitalizing on the dark and evil side of human nature: spoiling the elite in exchange for their loyalty.

With the understanding of these three realities, the communist officials developed an undocumented but almost unanimously accepted code of conduct-or rather, code of corruption. So, every piece of governmental power is on sale in the market and every corner of the market is invaded by political power.

Officials in all government agencies spent most of their energy beefing up GDP, engaging in power arbitrage, bribing their superiors, and seeking luxurious personal perks. As a result, the Communist Party elite, who used to label themselves "the vanguards of the proletariat class," had either turned themselves into get-rich-overnight capitalists, or become brokers, patrons, and backers of domestic and foreign capitalists.

In such a political environment, political power was dancing a full-swing tango with capital operation. Low human rights standards, low wages, lack of environmental protection regulations and enforcement, and the illegality of collective bargaining all contributed to creating a golden opportunity for domestic and international speculative capitalists. As a result, "money" quickly courted "political power." Business venture takers would go to any length to seek out someone in power to serve as backers so that they could grab market opportunities without fair competition. They also used political connections to shed any and all legal and social responsibility. In a sense, the Chinese Communist Party, which used to be China Inc.'s sole shareholder, had now opened up its equity and offered its shares for capitalists to purchase.

This is very important for one to understand why "the middle class prediction" has so far failed in China.

One. Given China's government-market relations, the middle class owed its success to the privileged relations with the state. To expect such a state-dependent class to make bold political claims would have been fanciful.

Two. Trade and economic development were carried out as a matter of deliberate state policy, unlike the US and UK these early developed countries which developed without knowing, the fast growth did not give rise to a politically independent middle class, but instead allowed the existing ruling structure to absorb into its own ranks the most talented and ambitious members of business elite. The CCP's 16th National Congress, for example, published a new Party Charter that welcomed capitalists as Party members.

Meanwhile, the shares of China, Inc. were offered to China's intellectuals as free, performance-related stock options. In order to sustain stability, the CCP regime offered all kinds of bribery incentives to buy off anyone and everyone of importance and influence in society. The bribery list includes bureaucrats at every level, military officers, and business leaders as well as college professors, journalists, publishers, authors, art performers, high-profile athletes, and so on. The government pays all these people off in the form of salaries, bonuses, state-covered expenses, free medical insurance, subsidized housing, free pension plans and so on. Laws and policies more and more favor this group of people in exchange for their recognition and acceptance of the political status quo. Their income and perks add up to wealth that is disproportionally higher than that of ordinary workers, farm workers, clerks, and small business owners. Such a policy of co-opting and buying off potential opposition was quite effective in conjunction with the purges and persecution after the Tiananmen massacre. The cruelty of political reality created terror in the minds of intellectuals as a psychological deterrent. As time went on, fear turned into the cynicism, they became increasingly indifferent to what was right and what was wrong. Indifference and hypocrisy rapidly became a new fashion that the modern Chinese intellect tried to follow. This, coupled with a piece of the action in China Inc., made many intellectuals-who had once been independent and once been considered the conscience of the society-soften up their position against the post-1989 status quo.

Over the 1990's and the first 10 years of the 21st century, in China, power (political elite), capital (economic elite) and "intellect" (social and cultural elite), were bonded together and formed an alliance that is maintaining the existing political order. This alliance owns and runs China, Inc., dazzling the entire world with its wealth, might and glory. With China's vast geographic size and population, the shareholders of China, Inc. have impressed many observers with their prodigious wealth accumulation and astonishing growth rates, making those same observers believe that one-party dictatorship is good for economic growth. By the same token, these shareholders also control all the channels of the information flow and dominate the public discourse. They can make their voices loud enough so the outside observers believe that they represent China, that they are China-the whole of China.

The truth is, there is another society named China, a society constituted of over a billion Chinese who are virtually laborers working for China, Inc. and whose basic rights are almost totally disregarded, the China that people sarcastically call "the China of shitizens."

This was the China's two-China structure I often talked about before Xi Jinping took the power. This was largely a two-player game.

During the same period, the US diplomatic establishment largely harbored the delusion that economic growth will bring about democracy in China. US Presidents and other senior officials, deeming human rights issues inconvenient while engaging with China, would avoid them as much as they could. Faced with the rising China, US gradually lost leverages. Now, the Chinese leadership practically cares little about the pressure from Western public opinion because politicians and businessmen from around the world are salivating at China's immense purchasing power, investment and markets. It's no exaggeration to say that today, Chinese leaders are the most well-received, honored guests in a majority of countries worldwide; China is the destination for many of the world's elite who thirst for gold.
Beijing tightly controls the freedom of the press. They could cut off Google and Yahoo anytime; they'd refused visas for New York Times journalists and critical scholars, and blocked access to Twitter and Facebook. All without impunity. While at the same time, they can set up any media they would like in the US. Ironically, China, which

screens, censors and bans any print and electronic publication, has been invited to serve as the country of honor at book fairs in Frankfurt, London, and New York! Hollywood is the epitome of free American culture; filmmakers are free to ridicule, mock, and criticize American politicians and government officials such as senators, judges, and the president, without fear of persecution. But in their pursuit of China's box office dollars, Hollywood executives have consciously decided to steer clear of any criticism of the Chinese government. Despite this, American movies are still censored in China, and some are not allowed at all. Virtually all American media are blocked in China. In the United States today, the Chinese government and its surrogates have wide access to universities, think tanks, and broadcast studios through which they can advance their opinions and rationalize their actions.

China is using the economic power it has gained with the help of the West to build a formidable, modern military. As its power grows, China is demanding a re-write of international norms and rules. China wants to create a new international order with China at the center of the Asia-Pacific region, bringing regional and world peace under threat. The current South China Sea tension is just a case in point.

In short, the failure of the US to proactively seek advancement of human rights and democracy in China has in turn harmed its long term national interest and its democratic way of life.

Let's look at China again to examine opportunities ahead of us.

Despite his unprecedented high-profiled anti-corruption effort, Xi Jinping has largely continued the two China structure and shown the world that he is more determined than his predecessors not to abandon the one-party dictatorship in favor of democratic reforms.

A subtle change, however, is taking place largely due to Xi Jinping's personality, anti-corruption campaign and the unstoppable economic down turn.

Xi Jinping has concentrated power in his own hands and built a cult of personality. The Economist writes that Xi is now not the CEO (the chief executive officer) but the COE, the "Chairman of Everything." He's the head of state, the leader of the Communist Party, the commander-in-chief of the armed forces, the head of the security services, the head of the committee in charge of the so-called "comprehensive reform," and also the person in charge of the economy.

He has abolished the practice of "collective leadership," which was adopted in 1982 to prevent a return to the totalitarian terror of Mao's unchecked dictatorship, which produced such horrors as the Cultural Revolution. All this has undergone through power struggles in form of anticorruption campaign. In doing so he has alienated his comrades at all levels and they have remained in a "state of idle" to quietly protest. One of the major reasons behind Xi's anticorruption campaign is the two-China ruling model-co-opting the elite and exchanging corruption for loyalty, has become increasingly costly and thus almost unbearable. But ending that model without granting people more liberties is an impossible task. The only thing it can achieve is to alienate the political, business, intellectual elite, the middle class if you will. With the economic down turn, more and more members of the middle class are feeling insecure and seeking to leave the ruling structure and even the country.

At the same time, Xi, acting out of fear, has overseen the harshest crackdown on dissent since the Tiananmen massacre, arresting lawyers, academics, workers, and civil society activists, and tightening controls over the media and access to the Internet.

Politically, the elite who are just beginning to turn their backs on the regime, are caught between a ruling party above, and a mass of workers and peasants below, with whom there is no mutual trust.

Xi Jinping is a game changer. He is unwittingly turning the two player game into a three player game, dissolving the power base that has helped the party stay in power to this day. This is the deepest crisis facing the Xi Jinping regime.

To be sure, growth is slowing; the party is in disarray, because the rules it has established to limit internecine political warfare have collapsed; Beijing's foreign policy is driving the Sino-U.S. relationship toward conflict; middle-class acquiescence is beginning to erode.

But I do not pretend that revolution will take place tomorrow.

We must be noted it usually takes four factors to be present at the same time to begin a real democratic transition in an autocratic country: 1) general robust disaffection from people; 2) split in the leadership in the autocratic regime; 3) viable democratic opposition; and 4) international support.

Let me elaborate.

First. China's Stability Sustaining System treats every citizen as a potential enemy, and it has successfully made them enemies–dissidents, independent intellectuals, land-lease peasants, victims of forced demolitions and eviction, victims of forced abortion, veterans, migrant workers, Tibetans, Uyghurs, Mongolians, Christians, and Falun Gong practitioners, you name it. The CCP regime does not lack enemies. With slower economic growth, the grievances of the shitizens will be laid barer and social unrests can only be mounting.

Second. As I said earlier, the elite China is beginning to decompose. Party's leadership unity has also disintegrated, as shown by the purge of Bo Xilai, Ling Jihua, Zhou Yongkang and their cronies since 2012.

Perhaps the only achievement in China's political system in the past 30 years is the establishment of the "two-term, 10-year, one-generation" term limit system. Many observers predicted that such a system would ensure long-term stability for the CCP regime, wishfully believing that this system helped the CCP find a way out of the pit of power discontinuity that has plagued all dictatorships in history. The Bo Xilai incident, however, mercilessly burst that bubble. Now it is Xi Jinping himself that is challenging this norm. The cracks within the party are only widening.

Third. The concept of democracy has prevailed in the minds of the general public, thanks to the dozens years of efforts made by the pro-democratic activists both in and outside of China.

In the meantime, the ordinary people are becoming more mature, more skillful, and more aggressive in fighting for their own civil rights. Generally speaking, as citizen forces grow and the civil protests escalate, struggle for power among different factions with the communist regime will become public. Especially, once the external pressure reaches a critical mass, the rivalry factions with the CCP will have to take the citizen force into serious account and seek or use the latter's support.

That said, I want to emphasize that we need an overall, viable pro-democracy movement to force the dictatorship to crack open. A milestone to meet that objective would be the formation of a group of civil leaders able to represent the general public, integrating the middle class and lower class people in demanding for democracy, and to at least partially disrupt the current political order — a group that will catch attention and support of the international community and can carry out and to call for effective negotiations with the government.

Fourth, last but not least, international support.

China under one-party dictatorship cannot rise peacefully, and its transition to a democratic country that respects human rights, rule of law, freedom of speech and religion, is in everyone's best interest, including America. In other words, the U.S. must push for a peaceful democratic transition in China. The reason for this is simple: To support

China's regime, a regime that ruthlessly represses its own people, denies universal values to justify its dictatorship, and challenges the existing international order to seek its dominance, is morally corrupt as well as strategically unsound. Like Frankenstein's monster, China is now seeking to revenge against its creator – the West.

While many policymakers in Washington have now realized that it is time to get tough on China, some still believe that the present and future conflicts between the U. S. and China can be managed. My view is this: Without China's democratization, a clash between the U. S. and China is unavoidable because the two countries' strategic goals are on a clashing course and their core interests cannot be compromised.

I hereby call the US to end the compartmentalization of human rights and begin to engage China with moral and strategic clarity.

To start, the Congress should pass a China Democracy Act that flatly states that enhancing human rights and democratic transition in China is decidedly in America's national interest and that directs the Federal government and all its agencies to make democracy and human rights advocacy the core of all engagement with China. This would be binding legislation precluding the currently widespread but inaccurate claim that Congress must balance, on the one hand, it's claim to support the universal value of human rights, and, on the other hand, "America's national interest." The bill also would require a report from the President to Congress every year on how any government program, policy, or action during the prior twelve months has strengthened or weakened human rights and democratic values in China.

All federal departments of government – every single one – should have to report on what they're doing to bring democracy to China by advancing human rights and the rule of law there. The Act also put them on notice to take no action, adopt no policy and implement no program that would undercut the democracy movement, or weaken human rights in China.

Such a China Democracy Act will give us a better idea of what successes we've had so far, what caused them, and how we should increase financial resources and deploy them to promote democracy and human rights.

Such an Act will serve as America's grand strategy toward China, setting a firm foundation that not only guides U. S. activities with China in all spheres, but also makes clear of the U. S. intentions to the Chinese government and sends an unequivocal message of support to the Chinese people.

No one can predict with precision when the moment of dramatic opening for change will come in China. Virtually every one of the sixty some peaceful transitions to democracy in the past few decades have come as a surprise to the US.

Above all else we must maintain our faith in my compatriots that they can and will join the vast majority of the world's peoples who now live in free or at least partly free countries. An opening for change could come in the next few months or it may take a few more years. But it will never come without collective efforts, including those from the international community. So we must persevere and keep the faith and be ready.

B.

New Approach to Take Back American Jobs while Advancing American Values

<u>Why America's China Policy has failed.</u> America may have won a few battles but it is losing the war, and its China policy has not worked by any standard in the past 30 years. The primary cause for the failure can be attributed to a fundamental misunderstanding of China's strategic intent, and a corresponding response with moral and strategic clarity. Regime security is the number one concern for China's Communist Party: it wants to maintain permanent rule of China's government, and replace capitalism with "socialism with Chinese characteristics", and replace Western civilization with Chinese civilization.

<u>We need an American-values focused foreign policy.</u> The Trump Administration must take a completely different approach in dealing with the Chinese regime by returning to an American-values focused foreign policy, and strike directly at the vulnerable spots of the regime to force China's democratic transition. A democratic China will avoid the inevitable conflicts with the U.S., and ensure a lasting peace in the region and the world.
We recommend the following specific actions:

1. Use the US market as leverage: withdraw China's permanent trade status and link it to political reform/human rights improvement, and de-militarization of South and East China Seas; deny foreign tax credit to companies that invest in the localities with gross human rights violation, and ban product imports from those localities; impose more restrictive export controls on dual use as well as surveillance technology, and other similar measures to address the unfairness of one-way free trade resulting in China's huge trade surplus of $3 trillion, and millions of American job lose, all of which will not only bring back jobs from China but allow the US to take the moral high ground.

2. Use Taiwan and Hong Kong as leverage: modify the Taiwan Act and the Six Assurances to reflect a full democratic country status and affirm its legitimacy by allowing Taiwan to be a normal member of the international community; support HK's struggle for universal suffrage by making it a major bilateral issue with China.

3. Use Japan as leverage: encourage Japan to take the lead in promoting democracy in Asia-Pacific and return it to the normal status of a great power.

4. Use the Chinese regime's lack of legitimacy and moral base as leverage: engage with China's democratic forces at a new level by passing the China Democracy Act to ensure all US government agencies are consistent in advancing a democracy agenda when engaging China, and by passing a China Defense of Human Rights and Civil Society Act, a China-specific Magnitsky-like legislation to ban travel and freeze assets of Chinese human right abusers, and pass the Act to rename the plaza in front of the Chinese embassy after imprisoned Nobel laureate Dr. Liu Xiaobo.

5. Use the UN human rights mechanisms as leverage: because both the Chinese government and its people take the UN as a legitimate world governing authority above the US, and the Chinese government has taken the UN as the stage on which it seeks to compete with the US to build a bi-polar world order in its own way, the Trump Administration must strengthen the US leadership role in forming an alliance of democracies to confront China on human rights collectively, and formulate a stronger human rights policy toward China that is consistent and cogent.

C.

Position Paper on Religious Freedom in China

The rapid growth of Christianity since the 1980s harbingers a profound change in the Chinese society. The Chinese government official data indicate there are 2300 million to 4000 million Christians in China. However, this number does not include the members of the Chinese house churches because the Chinese regime refuses to consider them as legitimate religious groups. If these Christians are counted, the total number of Chinese Christians could reach over 100 million. Some estimate believes that China is on its way to become the world's largest Christian country by 2030 with 240 million believers. Experts even predict that one third of China's population will convert to Christianity in next 30 years.

However, the Chinese Communist regime perceives the exponential increase of Christians to be a serious threat to its security and its permanent rule in China. They believe the Western reactionary force is using religion to infiltrate China and compete with the CCP for the people's minds and souls through ideological brainwash, ultimately leading to a color revolution to topple the regime.

While the regime leader Xi Jinping insists that all CCP members must be "unyielding Marxist atheists," he warns that "we must resolutely resist overseas infiltration through religious means and guard against ideological infringement by extremists." This perception made the regime shift the policy toward Christianity from "cautious management（谨慎管理）" to "proactive defense（积极防范)," attempting to change what the regime called "Primus Solus status" of one religion (一教独大） -- Christianity -- in China.

The Chinese regime has developed a comprehensive strategy in its attempt to reverse the trend. While the CCP continues to use persecution as a tool to instill fear in Chinese Christians, it has become much more sophisticated in employing other measures to respond to the rapid growth of Christianity in China. The strategy is summed up by Xi Jinping as "two goals and one means (两个目的和一个手段)." The first goal is to ensure the CCP's absolute control over all Christians; the second goal is to sinicize Christianity in order to thwart the West's attempt to use religion to "incite a color revolution." The CCP's "one means" is to use so-called "legal measures" to manage religions, which means they aim to control and ban underground Christian churches through the disguise of law.

First, the regime is using the newly passed China's National Security Law to "prevent, frustrate, and legally punish infractions of law and crimes conducted in the name of religious activities that compromise national security, resist overseas forces' intervention in domestic religious affairs, and maintain the normal order of religious activities (Article 27)." The regime brings all sorts of criminal charges against Christian practitioners; charges such as criminal "cult" activities, "gathering a crowd to disrupt public order" and "fraud" are arbitrarily brought against tens of thousands house church pastors, elders and congregants.

In parallel, the regime has launched a massive campaign to sinicize Christianity. This sneaky attack on Chinese Christians is extremely dangerous because it fundamentally and quietly alters Christian teachings to support the regime.

The essence of the sinicization is to remake Christianity and modify it in both doctrine and form into a religion without Jesus that will act as a tool to help strengthen the power grab of the CCP. According to the regime, the sinicization demands that all Christians to remain loyal to the CCP and obey its rule before they yield to God, that all Christians' activities must submit to the highest interests of serving the country, and that all Christian teachings must conform with the socialist core values and be interpreted accordingly. In addition, the architectural appearance of churches, worship rituals, music, and other religious practices must be replaced with Chinese elements.

To implement this strategy, Xi Jinping's confidant Xia Baolong, party chief of Zhejiang, initiated a campaign to crackdown the "illegal structures" of both house churches and TSPM churches in the province, resulting in over 1700 crosses on church buildings removed and demolished and at least 50 churches' entire buildings destroyed. Such campaigns have also been expanding to other provinces.

The sinicization campaign aims to brainwash Christians and to insert a subtle influence to change their mind and value orientation. The government agencies send task forces to churches to inculcate the "love CCP, love socialism" concept to the Christian believers. Meanwhile, the regime provides healthcare to church members, and offers financial support to the poor to win the believers' support.

The Chinese regime's aggressive campaign to remodel Christianity in China and its persecution of the Chinese Christians constitute a gross violation of international law. It will further jeopardize China's chance to transition into a democracy based on the Christian faith. Few in the Western world have realized the significance of China's assault on Christianity and Obama has been silent about the Chinese regime's abuses. We urge the Trump Administration, along with the support of America's evangelical community, to end the Chinese Communist regime's assault against Christianity.

We therefore recommend the following actions:

1. Reaffirm and highlight religious freedom as a core value that the United States will continue to advance and support in China, as one of the main objectives of U.S. foreign policy by raising the Office of International Religious Freedom to the bureau level in the State Department.
2. Make China's sinicization of Christianity and persecution of the Chinese Christians a primary factor that affects the U.S.-China bilateral relations, and raise these issues as the situation calls for whenever the two governments meet, particularly during the annual U.S.-China Consultation on People-to-People Exchange (CPE)
3. Condition China's permanent trade status with the termination of the sinicization of Christianity campaign and gross abuses of religion freedom.

4. Expand the people-to-people exchange program by adding religious components and increase its funding for more interactions between Chinese and American Christians.

5. Maintain a record for American Christian missionaries or workers to whom China denies visas and respond to unreasonable denials by reciprocating US visa issuance.

6. Increase the U.S. grants making for NGOs that advocate for religious freedom in China and demand the Chinese regime to suspend its implementation of the Foreign NGO Law.

* Dr. YANG Jianli, a Chinese Christian, Tiananmen Massacre survivor and former political prisoner, is the Founder and President of Initiatives for China/Citizen Power for China

Contact Info: Tele: 857-472-9039 Email:yangjianli001@gmail.com

PREPARED STATEMENT OF CHEN GUANGCHENG

DECEMBER 7, 2016

Greetings to the Chair people, to all the human rights Congressional representatives, ladies and gentlemen: Hello!

In China, people know me as, "the barefoot lawyer:" despite having no formal training as a lawyer, I did the work of a lawyer, bringing officials to court and asking that the party respect China's own Constitution and laws. As a result, I endured 7 years of kidnappings, house arrest, secret detention sites, and imprisonment. After I was let out of prison, my family and I were put under illegal house arrest under conditions even worse than prison, including torture, until I finally escaped.

My own experience tells me that one should not hold out any hope or possibility in the Communist Party. This is a fascist regime that destroys the essential goodness of humanity.

The Communist Party has been persecuting its own people for years. Last year it began the infamous 709 crackdown, persecuting human rights defenders and lawyers, torturing people and implicating family members by association. Some attorneys and activists in detention have been forced to make confess guilt in the state-controlled media, and have subsequently been sentenced to prison. But some, like Li Heping, Li Chunfu, Wang Quanzhang and other attorneys refuse to admit guilt, and hence continue to be held illegally. Two weeks ago, Attorney Xie Yang was tortured by prison police, and Attorney Jiang Tianyong has been disappeared. Activists Huang Qi and Liu Feiyue have been taken by public security. Countless netizens have been blocked online, and their speech censored.

Under Party control, the Chinese people have long lived in a state of suffering and fear. It should be clear that Communist authoritarian control is the enemy of humanity: we must put a stop to its destruction of humanity's civilized values.

On the other hand, America is a great nation that truly stands out in its commitment to universal values. There is simply no way to compare the US and China on this front. Hence, America must be a model for human rights, and a leader in the global push to democracy. The American system has the strongest immunity (against corruption), and the greatest capability for correcting its mistakes. Democracy, freedom, and human rights are America's founding principles. After many injurious years of appeasement and self-belittling, the time has come for the US to reinvigorate its core values and to protect universal human rights.

I would like to make the following recommendations to the incoming administration and Congress regarding human rights:

1. Correct the mistaken policy of separating trade from human rights. Human rights are like clean water, clean food, and clean air: they are an indispensable part of life, and cannot be separated from anything we do. The essence of the policy of separating trade and human rights is to focus solely on making money, without care to justice or ethics. In addition, the reality is that a country with strong human rights and rule of law is a better business partner for American companies.

2. In its position as a global leader, should express a position of clear support for the universal values of freedom, democracy, and human rights.When a dictatorial regime uses force to suppress its people, should act decisively to stop it. In addition, we should reconsider NATO's function, to transform NATO from hedgehog quill to heroic sword.

[NATO is now an organization primarily concerned with its own member nations and their security. The US should recognize that authoritarian regimes pose an existential threat to democracies everywhere. The US, for example, is already experiencing infiltration into many areas of civic and government life, including its media, academia, government offices, and electoral process by the largest dictatorships in the world. If this continues unabated, the US will find its democratic institutions substantially weakened. By supporting democratic movements through clear statements, the US and NATO will put a check to violent repression of innocent people and reclaim the importance of universal rights for all.]

3. Prevent human rights abusing officials from entering the United States. Investigate and where illegality is found, freeze the US assets of Communist Party officials.

4. Prevent the Communist Party from infiltrating US academia, media, and other institutions.

5. Demand that the Chinese Communist Party respect the UN International Treaty on Human Rights. Change the policy of speaking with the CCP on issues of human rights behind closed doors .otherwise we will continue the useless conversations we have now.

6. Ensure reciprocity of visas for journalists, and prevent the CCP from using visas to punish journalists who expose the crimes of the party.

[At the moment, the US allows roughly 800 journalists from China into the US, the majority of whom are from party media outlets, but China only allows 100 US journalists into China.]

7. Invest in tools to get past internet blocking mechanisms, to assist those who seek freedom in getting past the Great Firewall [Internet Berlin Wall]. Establish direct communication with the Chinese people, instead of just with the party.

8. Establish international, collaborative mechanisms to prevent the Chinese Communist Party from persecuting its own people internally, and from breaking down international procedures externally.

Great nations have great responsibility. In Chinese there is an ancient saying: "Bring out the best and eliminate the worst under heaven." This should be the principle to follow. As long as we join together, we can banish dictatorships, and make the world a better place.

Written by the 709 lawyers wives

The 709 Mass Arrest of Chinese Lawyers

As of today, one year and five months have passed since the mass arrest of lawyers orchestrated by the Chinese Communist Party since July 9, 2015 — an event now known as "the 709 incident."

Over 300 lawyers, human rights defenders, and legal assistants were summoned or arrested in the security mobilization, with over 20 individuals then subjected to criminal prosecution. Sentencing of the first batch was wrapped up in early August this year, in a series of anti-Western show trials, with Hu Shigen (胡石根), Zhou Shifeng (周世锋), Zhai Yanmin (翟岩民), and Gou Hongguo (勾洪国) being criminally sentenced on charges of "subversion of state power."

Li Heping (李和平), Wang Quanzhang (王全璋), Xie Yang (谢阳), Xie Yanyi (谢燕益), Li Chunfu (李春富), Wu Gan (吴淦), and other lawyers and human rights defenders are still in detention, and have been held in excess of the statutory limit. To this day there has still been no court date set, and recent reports from China indicate that Xie Yang, Li Heping, and other lawyers are being subjected to severe torture.

In the latest development, Jiang Tianyong (江天勇), another prominent human rights lawyer who has been campaigning for the release of the lawyers arrested last year, was himself disappeared on November 21. It's widely suspected that he has also been detained by Communist Party security forces.

In this last one year and five months, the arrested lawyers and rights defenders have been defended by officially-appointed counsel, depriving them of the right to have their families choose their own lawyers. In effect, this strips them of the right to defense. Wives of these lawyers then banded together to mount a continuous, lawful protest, demanding that their husbands be accorded the right to defense counsel. And yet the legitimate demands of the wives only led to Communist Party security officials following, harassing, monitoring, temporarily detaining, threatening, and beating them.

The 709 mass arrest of lawyers demonstrates that the Chinese Communist Party's claim of peaceful rise is nothing more than the further entrenchment and strengthening of totalitarianism, and runs in stark contradiction to the regime's own much-vaunted goal of building a country based on the rule of law. The Party instead uses ideas like the "China dream" and similar national-revival slogans to reinforce its political legitimacy, while deploying its formidable economic might to back a violent and forceful purge of domestic dissidents and the development of a powerful military.

If the international community doesn't wake up, it will soon see with its own eyes the rise of a Nazi-like neo-totalitarian state in Asia, one that will imperil the political security of both Asia and the world.

As demonstrated by the 709 lawyers, more and more Chinese people are waking up to their own civil rights, and they need more legal professionals to protect their property rights, personal freedom, and political rights. The strengthening of the community of rights defense lawyers in China will help the development of civil society, gradually expand the boundaries of freedom under the Party's high-pressure rule, and offer hope for continual improvements in the transparency of the Chinese political system and society.

There is no question that lawyers in China, as ably represented by those arrested during the 709 incident, are a crucial force that will determine whether China will make a successful political transition, and whether it will finally become a country based on universal principles of human rights.

For all these reasons, the international community should proactively expand its interactions with this force in China's civil society, work together to safeguard the personal freedom and right to practice of lawyers in China, and encourage the healthy development of civil society. This will fundamentally benefit the international balance of power and global security.

December 5, 2016

PREPARED STATEMENT OF BOB FU

RELIGIOUS FREEDOM AND RULE OF LAW UNDER XI JINPING 2016

DECEMBER 7, 2016

Dear Chairman Congressman Smith and Co-Chair Senator Marco Rubio,

As China regresses into a more Maoist regime, the Communist Party continues to place restrictive measures on human rights and religious freedom and executes its control over all forms of dissent by arresting or otherwise harassing those who oppose the strictures.

According to current president Xi Jinping, religion must conform to and benefit a socialist society. At a national conference on religion held in April of this year, he urged his administration to ensure that religions "merge religious doctrines with Chinese culture, abide by Chinese laws and regulations, and devote themselves to China's reform and opening up drive and socialist modernization in order to contribute to the realization of the Chinese dream of national rejuvenation," and argued that the role of the Party was to "guide and educate the religious circle and their followers with the socialist core values . . .."

His words reinforced a pre-existing nationwide crackdown on religious institutions, including an ongoing cross demolition campaign, arbitrary arrests of pastors and lawyers, and the suppression of Tibetan Buddhists and Uyghur Muslims. Because China Aid receives reports on Christian persecution, this summary will spotlight their cases as examples indicative of a much wider repression of belief.

In its 2015 Annual Report, *Chinese Government Persecution of Christians and Churches in China,* China Aid noted a 4.74 percent overall increase in persecution, based on how statistics gathered in 2015 compared to those collected the previous year. The various categories accounted for include: number of religious persecution cases (up 10.84 percent), number of persecuted individuals (up 8.62 percent), number of unjustly detained persons (up 6.14 percent), number of abuse cases (up 174.65 percent) and number of abused people (up 91.32 percent).

Persecution campaigns made 2016 one of the most tyrannical years since the Cultural Revolution. As imprisoned human rights lawyers still fight for the right to defend their clients without legal repercussions, officials in Zhejiang province carry out the third consecutive year of a beautification movement that targets church crosses for demolition, Henan province launched a movement focusing on forcing "illegal" Catholic and Protestant churches to conform to socialist ideals, and authorities arrested and detained church members.

Trials for lawyers rounded up in the 709 incident, the nationwide crackdown on human rights defenders named for the day it started, July 9, 2015, commenced on August 2 with the sentencing of Zhai Yanmin, a rights activist who received a three-year suspended prison term for coordinating protests against government rule. A day later, a Tianjin court condemned Beijing church elder Hu Shigen to seven-and-a-half-years' incarceration and five years' deprivation of political rights for allegedly "subverting state power" by using Christianity to "spread subversive thoughts and ideas." The tribunal presented photos of his baptism as evidence of his guilt, and Hu was forced to confess to his crimes, after which he accepted his sentence and did not appeal.

Hu, a Beijing University alumnus and former instructor at the Beijing Language Institute, formerly served 16 years of a 20 year prison sentence for founding an organization that opposed the Communist Party.

On August 4, Zhou Shifeng was coerced into confessing to his crimes. Zhou, a Christian attorney, was arrested on suspicion of "subverting state power" on January 8, 2016. In an attempt to publicly authenticate their charges against him, authorities pressured Zhang Kai, a human rights lawyer known for his defense of more than 100 churches affected by the cross demolition campaign, to travel from his home in Inner Mongolia, attend the trial, and conduct an interview in which he denounced Zhou and the other imprisoned human rights lawyers. Zhang later recanted his statements, saying he had been too frightened to stand up to the authorities. Consequentially, officials barred him from social media and attempted to arrest him again.

On the night of August 25, 2015, government personnel broke into a church in Wenzhou, Zhejiang and took Zhang and his two legal assistants into police custody. After holding him incommunicado for six months in an unofficial prison known as a "black jail," China forced Zhang to confess on television on February 25, 2016. A few days later, he was taken into criminal detention and released on bail on March 23. Since then, he has lived with his parents in Inner Mongolia.

Another Christian lawyer, Li Heping, vanished into police custody on July 10, 2015, followed by his brother, attorney Li Chunfu, on August 1 of that year. Li Heping was formally arrested on January 8, 2016, on suspicion of "subverting state power." Since their disappearance, family members have not been able to contact either of the men.

The cross demolition movement, which began in 2014 as part of a beautification campaign known as "Three Rectifications and One Demolition," continued in Zhejiang province during 2016. Although official rhetoric claims the operation intends to address "illegal structures," it specifically discriminates against Christian churches and imposes strictures on the crosses that adorn the exterior of their buildings. In 2016, the number of crosses demolished surpassed 1,800.

Zhang Chongzhu, a pastor who was placed under "residential surveillance in a designated location," otherwise known as a "black jail," in September 2015, was originally held in police custody for his opposition to the cross demolitions,. On February 5, he was criminally detained for "stealing, spying, buying, or illegally providing state secrets or intelligence to entities outside China." He was formally arrested on March 9 for the same crime. On May 9, he was released.

Now, Zhang faces a new challenge; on October 29, the Zhejiang Provincial China Christian Council and the Zhejiang Provincial Three-Self Patriotic Movement, China's two state-run Christian organizations, expelled him from the clergy and revoked a certificate proving that he was licensed to preach. This triggered outrage among local Christians, one of whom speculated that the government terminated Zhang Chongzhu in order to keep citizens from attending house churches.

In addition to previous restrictions on religious activity, Henan province published a work plan devising to bring "illegal" Catholic and Protestant churches in line with the Party's ideologies. According to the official document, the authorities plan to manage church meetings and force the congregations to eradicate all religious symbols and become more socialist. The timeline outlined by the official document stated the plan was to be implemented on September 4 and run until October 15. The government mandated that the village and sub-district government branches investigate churches, submit reports to their superiors, assist the religious affairs bureau in distributing a notice about the expected changes to the churches, shut down non-compliant congregations, and record how satisfactorily they were able to complete the job as part of their year-end assessment.

Prompted by this decision, the Bo'Ai County Religious Affairs Bureau issued a notice to a house church. Claiming that the church was unauthorized, the bureau ordered it to immediately disband and remove any religious materials within three days. They urged the attendees to conduct religious activities at the local official churches, with which many of them have deep, theological disagreements. Failure to comply with these measures will result in further government interference.

This campaign echoes the new political trend set out in a proposed revision of the Regulations on Religious Affairs, which was introduced by the State Council earlier this month. The revision introduces tighter control on peaceful religious activities, such as punishing house church meetings by imprisoning Christians or heavily fining the church leaders, forbidding religious adherents from attending conferences or trainings abroad, and barring minors from receiving religious education. By passing these regulations, China violates its own Constitution, which guarantees religious liberty and condemns discriminating against religious and non-religious citizens, and breaches the country's pledges to adhere to the Universal Declaration of Human Rights, the International Covenant on Civil and Political Rights, and the United Nations' Convention on the Rights of the Child.

Paraphrasing and quoting an unnamed expert on the Regulations on Religious Affairs, Christianity Today published the following statements on October 3 in an article entitled "Red Tape: China Wants to Constrict Christian Activities with 26 New Rules," referring to China's State Administration on Religious Affairs as SARA:

> The draft law opens with the assurance that all Chinese citizens are free to believe whatever they want and to engage in religious activity—as long as it's within the tighter limits. One Chinese religious policy expert, who asked to remain anonymous, summed up some of what the regulations include:
>
> • No religious activities that are not approved by SARA.
>
> • No one may provide a venue for religious services that are not approved by SARA.
>
> • No one may use their home for religious practices that are not approved by SARA (including home or family Bible studies).
>
> • No publishing religious materials without approval from SARA.

- No foreign or domestic donations may be made to any religious organization that hasn't been approved by SARA.
- No one may call themselves a pastor without the approval of SARA.
- No international religious exchanges may happen without the approval of SARA.
- No one may study theology at school without the approval of SARA.

"As you can imagine, these amendments to the administration of religion in China by SARA would in effect leave no space for the house or unregistered church in China, and will significantly curtail many of the activities of the TSPM [Three-Self Patriotic Movement] as well," the expert told ChinaSource.

In 2015, a major developing case emerged as authorities increased pressure on Huoshi Church, the largest house church in Guiyang, Guizhou province. Though preluded by a police presence when the church moved into a new building in 2014 and the 2015 arrest of Zhang Xiuhong, an accountant and chairwoman at the church who was apprehended when she withdrew church funds at her beauty shop, the situation escalated when Pastor Su Tianfu received an administrative penalty notice on October 21, 2015. It indicted himself, Zhang and a church member named Liang Xuewu for "changing usage plans" of the office space the church rents for its services and ordered them to stop holding religious activities there, despite the church continually reporting its services to the government. Originally, the building was approved for business operations. When they neglected to heed the orders, officials imposed a fine that accumulated 12,960 Yuan (U.S. $2,030) daily.

Su, who is currently released on bail, has been under constant surveillance since December 19 and must use government-arranged transportation for all outings. He is expected to stand trial soon.

Additionally, administrative offices dispatched uniformed and plainclothes personnel to raid the church on several occasions. On December 9, 2015, Pastor Li Guozhi, better known by his alias, Yang Hua, was taken into police custody and sentenced to two consecutive, five-day administrative detention terms a day later for the "crime of obstructing justice" and "gathering a crowd to disturb public order" after he attempted to prevent officials from confiscating a church hard drive. When his wife came to collect him on December 20, she witnessed him donning a black hood and being herded into an unlicensed vehicle. Upon further inquiry, she learned that her husband had been charged with "illegally possessing state secrets" and was being transferred to another facility for criminal detention. She was not allowed to contact him. On January 22, she received a notice announcing his formal arrest and changing his charge to "divulging state secrets."

Even with his impending trial, which is expected to take place this month, authorities only permitted Yang to convene with his lawyers beginning in March. During one meeting, lawyer Chen Jiangang and his co-counsel, Zhao Yonglin, noted that he appeared fearful and began to suspect that he had been tortured. On their next visit, Zhao transcribed an interview with Yang in which he described how the prosecutors assigned to his case had stepped on his toes and threatened to kill him and harm his family in order to extract a confession from him. After hearing this, Chen and Zhao filed a lawsuit against the prosecution team and asked that they be criminally punished for "using torture to extort a confession."

During one of his pre-trial meetings, Yang requested that Zhang Wei, one of the prosecutors in his case, be disqualified from hearing the trial on account of his torture allegations. Chen and Zhao have furthered this request by submitting a document requesting both the disqualification of Zhang and a transferal to a new court. In the highest profile case of Christian persecution since the Cultural Revolution, China ousted Gu Yuese, chairman of the Hangzhou branch of the China Christian Council, from his position as the head pastor of China's largest Three-Self Church on January 18. Later that month, Gu was arrested on a falsified charge of "embezzling 10 million Yuan (US$1.6 million) in funds," although many Christians believe authorities incarcerated him for his opposition to the cross demolition campaign. On April 1, he was released and placed under "residential surveillance." His case demonstrates the rampant spread of religious persecution as China clamps down on both house and state-run churches.

As 2016 progressed, religious persecution continued to intensify. In Xinjiang, a politically and ethnically restive region wrought with religious tension, authorities apprehended dozens of Christians in the last two months. One of them, Ma Huichao, was taken from her home in September, where she and four other Christians were gathering for a church service. As a result of the service, she was charged with "gathering a crowd to disturb public order," and her trial of the first instance commenced in mid-November. According to Li Dunyong, her defense attorney, he was barred from pleading innocent on her behalf. Currently, the court is adjourned.

Recently, two Hong Kong residents, Lin Haixin and his wife, vanished into police custody for running a church that specialized in offering assistance to individuals suffering from addictions and mental health problems. The church was raided, and officials confiscated its computer and religious materials, banned it from holding religious services and dispersed Christians gathered there.

For two days, local Christians tried unsuccessfully to contact them. Some speculate that they were taken away for holding so-called "illegal religious activities" without registering.

Concerns over the safety of human rights lawyers spiked in the past weeks as Jiang Tianyong, a prominent human rights lawyer turned activist following his disbarment in 2007, disappeared, believed detained. He contacted his wife shortly before boarding a train from Changsha to Beijing, after which no one has been able to successfully reach him. He had been returning from a trip to visit the wife of Xie Yang, another human rights lawyer who was imprisoned during the lawyer crackdown last year, and helped her petition for his release. In the past, Jiang has been incarcerated for his work and suffered torture at the hands of the authorities.

On the morning of November 29, the brother of veteran human rights activist Peng Ming received a call from prison authorities saying that Peng had suddenly collapsed while watching television and was found dead. However, three days ear- lier, Peng had received a visit from his brother, who reported that the prisoner was in satisfactory health. When he arrived at the hospital and tried to place a call to his sister, who lives in California, officials took the phone from him and related their version of the story. Peng's family has since demanded an autopsy to confirm the cause of his death, and the Chinese government has warned them not to travel to China for the funeral.

At the time of his death, Peng was serving a lifelong prison sentence that began on May 28, 2004, when Chinese agents lured him into Burma while he was visiting his parents in Thailand and abducted him. After arriving in China, he was charged with leading a terrorist organization and kidnapping and possessing counterfeit money and given a life sentence. Upon investigation, the U.N. Working Group on Arbitrary Detention concluded in 2005 that authorities arbitrarily detained Peng, violating his right to freedom of expression and association.

China is unwilling to commit to furthering religious freedom and human rights, which caused both a significant demise of human rights under the Xi Administration. Western policies can hold the country accountable for abuses of basic freedoms.

It is time for the West to shift their paradigm from appeasing China to truly principled engagement. Like what happened before in the West during Hitler's rule of Germany in the 1930s, the current policy of ignoring China's anti-democratic system of governance in pursuit of economic opportunity will likely produce irreparable damage for the fundamental interests of the free world.

Recommendations:

I urge the Trump Administration and members of Congress, including President Trump himself, to meet with religious leaders and family members of prisoners of conscience and visit religious sites- especially churches, mosques and Tibetan Buddhism temples when visiting China in order to:

1. Raise cases not only behind doors, which has proved non-effective so far, but in public as well. Look at what happened to the prompt release of the "China feminist 5" after interventional outcry, including public demands by Secretary John Kerry and United States Ambassador to the United Nations Samantha Power.

2. Use multi-faceted approaches to religious freedom and human rights. The "human rights dialogue" mechanism has failed, be it bilateral or multilateral. After all, FoRB is a universal value. If the Chinese regime only sees the West as interested in talking about this issue behind closed doors in a compartmentalized way, it's nothing but a green light for the abuses to continue.

3. Adopt a concerted, internationally coordinated effort by working jointly with our allies in Europe and other regions. The release of imprisoned human rights lawyer Zhang Kai and Pastor Wen Xiaowu, who were freed after the Communist Party received enormous international pressure, are good examples of how well this method works.

4. Pressure China to stop committing violations of international law by overstepping their own nation's boundaries to detain dissidents such as Jiang Yefei and Dong Guangping, who were taken back to China from a detention center in Thailand; Peng Ming, who was kidnapped after being

lured into Burma by Chinese special agents and died on November 29 while serving a life sentence; and five Hong Kong booksellers, who disappeared into police custody for selling gossip books about the private lives of Chinese officials.

In conclusion, China continuously violates its own laws and international statutes safeguarding religious freedom and human rights in favor of promoting a socialist agenda, forcing dissidents and religious devotees to choose between certain persecution and disregarding their deeply-held beliefs. Additionally, it prosecutes lawyers who attempt to defend the rights of religious practitioners and activists, completely disregarding the rule of law. International governments must publicly and proactively organize efforts to persuade China to free those it unjustly holds behind bars and refrain from unproductive, behind-closed-doors conversations on these matters. Should the international community fail to do this, they will be communicating to China that they care more about trade than human rights, permitting these abuses to continue.

SUGGESTIONS ON THE FUTURE SINO-US ECONOMIC AND
TRADE RELATIONS AND THE REASONS

PREPARED STATEMENT OF WEI JINGSHENG

DECEMBER 7, 2016

When Donald Trump becomes president of the USA, he is planning to abolish the TPP and began a trade war with China in order to save the US economy. Some people say that this is a disaster, I would say that this is the right way that should have started even earlier. The reality after sixteen years well explain my position: granting China permanent MFN status, that is PNTR, was a huge mistake. It did not promote the development of the US economy, but was a blood transfusion from the USA to the Chinese economy. It gave China the opportunity to engage in trade war with the United States.

The reason is as follows. The so-called free trade, refers to a unified law based on the domestic market, thus allowing free trade. Such free trade can be carried out normally between countries with similar legal systems. There cannot be normal free trade between countries with completely different legal systems.

For example, after trade with China liberated, there were two main problems: one was cheap labor, one was its uncertain laws that always change.

Since Chinese law does not guarantee human rights, it is able to keep labor prices at a very low level. This has led to the relocation of US companies to foreign countries, while also allows Chinese goods entering the US market with low prices, resulting in unfair competition. It is an important cause of unemployment in the United States.

China's precarious legal system creates serious non-tariff barriers. Any local government can develop their own laws and regulations, without the need to implement the signed treaties and agreements between the Chinese central government and foreign countries. So they can actually close their targeted import market. Coupled with the manipulation of the currency by the Chinese central government, these actions increased exports and created a huge trade surplus for China. This is an important reason causing the economic recession in the USA.

Some people say: for the USA, fighting a trade war with China will end in defeat, at best a lose-lose result. I think such statements are to confuse the US policy makers. I think the USA will win this trade war, while China can only succumb to the rules developed by the United States, otherwise it will accelerate the collapse of the Chinese Communist regime. My reasons are as follows.

First: Now the vast majority of goods are in the buyers' markets. The United States holds the markets, thus it has the power to develop rules, instead of forcing itself to comply with that so-called global free trade rule that cannot be enforced. The United States can formulate its own fair trade rules, to replace the invalid so-called free trade rules.

Second: The Chinese domestic market is narrow and cannot afford the disaster of losing the US market. So China can only compromise on the rules thus to protect part of the market share.

Third: In the past, due to over-expansion of export production of shoddy goods, the quality of Chinese enterprises is very poor. In order to adapt to a fair market in the competition, Chinese companies must quickly upgrade. Thus there will be a great demand for technology and services from the United States to open up the import market in the USA. This will help expand US exports and reduce its trade deficit with China.

Fourth: After improving human rights in China, the income of the Chinese working class will increase, therefore the domestic consumer market will expand. This expansion would benefit US exporters after fair trade, thereby reducing the US trade deficit and even eliminating it.

So I think that the USA will win this trade war, and in the long run will also be beneficial to the economic normalization in China. China must accept and should accept it.

Thank you!

———

PREPARED STATEMENT OF REBIYA KADEER

DECEMBER 7, 2016

Since my release from a Chinese prison in 2005, I have reported to the Commission the continuing human rights violations targeting the Uyghur people. As the Commission has noted in its annual reports, political freedoms in East Turkestan are among the most limited in China. The right to association and assembly is prohibited and freedom of speech is punished severely, as the case of imprisoned Uyghur academic Ilham Tohti illustrates. Economic discrimination, erosion of language rights and religious restrictions add to the already depressing condition of Uyghur human rights.

President Xi Jinping has attempted to codify these violations in a series of repressive laws, such as the ones on counter-terror and cybersecurity. Implementation measures of the counter-terror law at the regional level in East Turkestan are a clear indicator of who China intends to target with these draconian measures.

Nevertheless, China believes it should go further with its repression. Arbitrary detentions, forced disappearance and extra-judicial killings continue. Recent media reports indicate the Chinese government has implemented a policy to confiscate passports in East Turkestan to limit the international movement of Uyghurs. This is the formalization of a policy that Uyghur human rights groups have documented since 2006.

Islam is a cornerstone of the Uyghur identity. China has adopted a series of religious laws at the national and regional level (2015) that curb Uyghur rights to freedom of worship. Private communal religious education has been targeted for several years under these measures; however, this year Chinese authorities adopted rules to report parents who encourage their children to undertake religious activities

During the George W. Bush and Barack Obama administrations my colleagues and I have worked hard to bring Uyghur issues to the attention of the U.S. political community. Our organizations regularly brief State Department officials and legislators at the U.S. Congress. We have managed to mainstream the Uyghur issue into U.S. government reporting on human rights.

Most notably, I was privileged to meet President George Bush on two occasions; the first time in June 2007 and the second in July 2008. These meetings placed Uyghurs at the center of U.S. policy concerns over human rights in China.

China's heavy handed policies towards Uyghurs are creating instability and desperation among the Uyghur people. These policies have become self-fulfilling in some respects, as some Uyghurs have become radicalized in their effort to oppose China's repression. The United States should be concerned about these developments as it is in the nation's interest to support the democratic aspirations of the overwhelming majority of Uyghurs. Stability in East Turkestan, China and the Central and East Asian regions offers the opportunity to spread American values such as freedom and rights.

The administration of President-elect Donald Trump should continue support for Uyghur democrats and step up public concern over rights conditions in East Turkestan with Chinese officials. Any sign that the United States is ready to relinquish its commitment to raising human rights concerns in favor of achieving policy gains elsewhere will be a victory for China.

Furthermore, the incoming administration should exercise extreme skepticism regarding China's narrative that increased militarization and securitization in East Turkestan are justified in fighting radical Islam. The repression that accompanies security measures enables China to keep firm control of the region and suppress legitimate Uyghur claims for greater political, economic, social and cultural freedoms. The Trump administration should understand the situation in East Turkestan in similar terms to the Tibet. It is a struggle for cultural survival in the face of formidable assimilative actions by the state.

Let us be clear. Pressure works. My presence here today is testament to the success of pressurizing Chinese officials. My colleagues and I will continue to put forward the Uyghur case to the international community. It is the responsibility of concerned governments to take this case directly to China and urge reform. The Uyghur people greatly appreciate the United States' support of our plight.; however, we ask the incoming administration to publicly raise the Uyghur issue with China.

In conclusion, I offer these recommendations to the Trump administration:

1. Prioritize Uyghur issues, especially during the Human Rights Dialogue and the Strategic and Economic Dialogue.

2. Urge China to allow foreign diplomats and journalists unrestricted access to East Turkestan to independently document the conditions in the region.

3. Call on China to free Ilham Tohti and his students and all writers and reporters.

4. Ask China to change its repressive policy, which is root cause of all bloody incidents in Uyghur region.

5. Meet Uyghur leaders and activists at the White House.

6. Create a special coordinator office at the State Department for the Uyghurs.

Congressional-Executive Commission on China (CECC) Hearing "Dissidents Who Have Suffered for Human Rights in China: A Look Back and A Look Forward"

Personal Statement by Xiaodan Wang
December 5, 2016

Thank you for having me as a part of this important hearing. While I am grateful to be here to speak, I am also heartbroken because it means the persecution against Falun Dafa has not ended and my father, Zhiwen Wang, is still not truly free.

2017 will mark the 18th year of persecution, the 18th year my father has been subject to cruel, unjust, and unfair treatment, and the 18th year I have been trying to bring my father home to freedom.

Growing up, my father was my home. He was safety and warmth for me. No matter how busy he was he would ride his bike home from work to make lunch for me. Every day he put me before himself and protected me from the communist influence of society.

We began practicing self-cultivation through Falun Dafa together. With its five exercises and principles of truthfulness, compassion, and tolerance, our hearts became brighter and we felt that we had found true happiness in letting go of pursuits and desires. My home was full of joy as excited practitioners came by to share their experiences with the practice. Some spoke of personal conflicts they had resolved while others had experienced massive health improvements. Looking back, these things were truly incredible and yet so common. Had I known better, I would have tried to soak in every smiling face and cherish every fleeting moment for they would soon be plunged into darkness.

Although it was difficult for my father to see me go to the United States, he has always wanted the best for me. I parted from him in 1998 without the slightest awareness it would be the last time I would see him for more than a decade and a half.

In the year that followed, we kept in touch every week on the phone. In early 1999, my father mentioned that some things had been happening with the government, but he never doubted they would be peacefully resolved.

In April of 1999, thousands of practitioners gathered near the government headquarters in Beijing to voice their concern that they had been mistreated. My father was not even present until he received a call that someone from the government wanted to speak to some practitioners. Since he had been practicing for a long time and had helped setup some of the Falun Dafa seminars, they called him to the meeting. By all counts, it seemed the meeting went well and practitioners would not be bothered for practicing anymore.

Had it not been for Jiang Zemin, this may have been true.

When this peaceful appeal happened in April 1999, Jiang, as leader of the Chinese communist party (CCP), made it his mission to destroy the practice. The mandate from him and his faction towards practitioners was to "ruin their reputations, bankrupt them financially, and destroy them physically." Think of what an absurd direction for a government to have toward its own citizens! On top of that, these were upstanding people like my father who contributed his best work to his job and volunteered so much of his time to helping others become healthier, better people.

In July of 1999, the curtain descended upon China and everything that was bright and good was covered in horrifying persecution. My father was dragged from his home and disappeared for months without a trace. It wasn't until December that he was put on a show trial and sentenced in front of the world on live TV for crimes he never committed. He couldn't defend himself as he was in a courtroom run by the same regime that was driving the persecution!

I could do nothing but cry. I was suffocating in despair as I watched my kind, good father being sentenced to 16 years in prison. As a practitioner of Falun Dafa, we strive to overcome hardships and endure with kindness. I could feel this darkness was trying to destroy that hope and that light within me. This feeling went on for what felt like an eternity until I came to the realization that I must stand up for him and put all my effort into ending the persecution.

For fifteen years I called for help, attended rallies, went to international events, met with government officials, and took interviews with the media. In my heart, I only wanted my father's suffering to end and for him to be released early. That day came on October 18, 2014, but rather than going home, the regime sent him to a brainwashing facility. It was as if the 15 years in prison had not been enough – as if the stroke he suffered in September of that year had not caused enough damage. They still wanted to break him down further.

When he finally made it home it was to video surveillance and neighborhood watch programs. Police regularly visited and on "sensitive days" he was advised to stay home and out of sight. By no means had he truly returned to a normal life, but given his grace and kindness as a Falun Dafa practitioner, he had let go of any ill feelings and bore no grudges against those who had mistreated him. Despite the regime's relentless effort to break his spirit, he remained with truthfulness, compassion, and tolerance guiding his life. He lived under constant pressure for a year and a half until he received his passport in January 2016. That was when we thought and hoped a new chapter would begin.

In July of this year, my husband and I traveled to China to escort my father through the legal immigration process. He had all his documents in order and a new passport ready to go. What should have been a straightforward trip became a nightmare of spying, intimidation, and harassment.

To even meet with my father, he had to evade the constant monitoring of three newly installed agents outside his home in Beijing. Although we were on edge, we had to keep moving forward. Of course we were not doing anything wrong, but from the very start it felt like they were trying to get under our skin.

On August 1st, we managed to fly from Beijing all the way to Guangzhou in the south without incident, but as soon as we went for his medical examination we were being monitored. On August 4th, we went to pick up his medical results and go to his immigration interview at the U.S. Consulate in Guangzhou. From the moment we entered the medical facility, my father's photo was taken and the spying was set in motion. After we had the medical results we went to a nearby Starbucks to wait for the interview. In that short time, multiple agents cycled in and out of the store to take our photo.

We went to the Consulate next and it was crowded with people standing around. A network of spies and undercover agents are stationed around the U.S. Consulate in Guangzhou and we even saw some agents coming out from the Consulate gate marked "Federal Tax Agency 国税局." There were unmarked Buick minivans stationed on the street in front of the building and undoubtedly there were agents watching everyone who came and went.

After years of being crammed into small jail cells with other inmates and being watched constantly, my father is very sensitive to being watched. After our successful immigration interview we were followed by car and on foot. When we exited our taxi over a mile from the Consulate, there were undercover agents watching us almost immediately. My father was the first to notice an agent taking his photo. It got to the point that I had to confront the undercover agents so my dad and husband could leave without being followed. We thought we had made it back without being followed, but there was a suspicious man waiting in the lobby where we were staying when we got back as well.

The next day, we noticed more suspicious things happening. As I left to pickup the approved immigration visa, I saw two "electricians" and a building security man were acting strange in the hallway. After I was gone, my husband saw one of them trying to look into our place through the peephole and under the door. Later that night a group of 10 police and undercover agents showed up at our door, trying to force their way in. There were another 20 officers and agents on street level. The police made up various excuses as to why they were there, but it was clear that their goal was to take away my father. We refused to let them in and my husband called the consulate for help. Eventually the police and agents relented, but we felt extremely unsafe there.

The next day we left for Dongguan, south of Guangzhou, to take a ferry to Hong Kong to fly home. We left early in the morning and were immediately followed. Even after driving 1.5 hours on the highway, spies were waiting for us at the ferry terminal. When we tried to exit through customs, they said my father's passport had been canceled and they cut the corner off. This destroyed the usefulness of the passport, but also shattered everything we had worked so hard for over the past 17 years. Despite the tremendous pressure, stress, and uncertainty, my father told me that we must not blame them and we must carry ourselves like practitioners. I am still humbled by my father's steadfast belief and genuine embodiment of the principles of Falun Dafa.

Ultimately, we were forced again by the communist regime to separate. This time I had to let my father go off alone into the uncertain and terrifying world of persecution. As his daughter who had come to rescue him from nearly two decades of living under such terror, misinformation, and hate, I had to leave him over a thousand miles from his home to walk his path without support. Tears rained down as I watched him disappear into that dark, cruel hallway. As I looked for him out the window, I wondered in agony why in such a huge country there isn't one small space for my father to live. Why is there no room for him to breathe? After all that he has suffered, why can't they just let him go?

Although my father had served fifteen years in prison that he never should have had to, that wasn't enough for the regime. As a so-called "supplementary punishment," he was denied political rights for four years lasting until 2018. While this does not bar him from travel, the regime uses the ambiguity of the concept to do whatever it wants with former prisoners. Now that my father has returned home to Beijing, there are agents literally camping outside his front door 24 hours a day. While he may not be in prison, he is monitored and followed as if he was. This is entirely an extension of persecution against him as a Falun Dafa practitioner.

This will be the fourth presidential administration I have come to ask for help. I believe the help we have received from the U.S. government has gotten us to this point, but we need a final push to bring my father to the U.S. where he can live in true freedom for the first time in his life.

But this story is not only about my father as there are approximately 100 million Falun Dafa practitioners in China suffering this inhumane persecution. In addition, the monstrous, state-run organ harvesting operation continues its coldblooded victimization of practitioners. This is evil that the world has not come to terms with yet, but every moment wasted costs more lives and destroys more families. Given how many lives have been lost through the persecution and the clear documentation of organ harvesting, there is not a minute to lose in condemning the CCP and its actions until it stops. History has proven that an improved economy has not improved the human rights situation in China. Only constant attention, pressure, and exposure will bring about better human rights for the people of China.

Not everyone in the CCP believes the persecution against Falun Dafa is correct, nor did the standing members of the Politburo agree with it before it began. Even today, it is Jiang Zemin's faction that struggles to maintain control of the CCP and keep the persecution in motion. We believe it was Jiang's right hand, Zeng Qinghong, and his group that are concentrated around Guangzhou that interfered with my father traveling abroad. We hope that the good people in China against the persecution will continue to step forward and work towards ending this crime against humanity.

In terms of concrete actions that are possible for the U.S. government and incoming administration, I would suggest

1. the new president to meet with a group of activists and torture survivors from China, including Falun Gong, even before the inauguration. The diverse and inclusive list of witnesses of this hearing could be a good starting place.
2. the U.S. Government bar entry to any official who could reasonably be considered to have been involved in the decision to deny Zhiwen Wang's exit from China – especially Zeng Qinghong and his cohorts.
3. members of congress who go to China or meet with Chinese officials to check the CECC political prisoner database and be ready with the name of at least one Falun Gong prisoner from the official's province or city to raise with the official.
4. the President, State Department and relevant departments to use all means to bring my father to the U.S. safely as he is already an approved U.S. immigrant and only needs to arrive here to finalize paperwork.
5. to continue escalating the investigation into the persecution and organ harvesting until all facts have surfaced and criminals are brought to justice.

There is no doubt that human rights continues to be an extremely severe issue that must be constantly addressed with the Chinese regime in an open and public way. When the regime manages to take the conversation from public view, it then spins it into a notion that the U.S. has no problem with China's human rights record and therefore everything is ok. My father, husband, and I can all testify that the persecution against Falun Dafa practitioners is very real and is ongoing.

I hope that this issue will continue to escalate and pressure will mount until the regime relents and redresses Falun Dafa and practitioners after all the damage it has done not only to them, but also to the entire society. Falun Dafa practitioners will continue to expose this crime against humanity within China and around the world, but a chorus of voices from governments around the world starting with the United States as a human rights champion will accelerate the end of the persecution. I truly hope the U.S. government can play a stronger and stronger role in the time ahead so that not only my family will be made whole again, but so will all practitioners with families shattered by this terrible injustice.

Thank you.

Prepared Statement of Hon. Christopher H. Smith, a U.S. Representative From New Jersey; Chairman, Congressional-Executive Commission on China

This has been another dark and difficult year for Chinese rights defenders and democracy activists. Under President Xi Jinping's version of the rule by law, the law is being used to more severely curb the freedom of expression, civil society, religious freedom, and other fundamental rights.

Chinese courts have convicted rights activists and lawyers of "subversion of state power" for simply seeking to represent religious groups, petitioners, and democracy advocates.

China's diverse religious communities faced even more restrictions, as new regulations, and a "sinicization" campaign, will further politicize religious life and lead to more repression.

In Hong Kong, mainland China's political interference and its abduction of booksellers threatens the rule of law and Hong Kong's promised autonomy, contributing to a growing climate of insecurity.

Internationally, China continues to push a relativistic version of human rights, characterizing universal values as "Western" values that do not apply to China's national situation.

The next Administration faces major challenges in dealing with China. A new approach is needed that learns the lessons of the past and listens to those who have suffered prison and persecution to advance fundamental freedoms in China.

The problem is that U.S. diplomacy is stuck with policies that no longer match Chinese realities. For the past two decades, U.S. policy was based on the belief that China's growing prosperity would bring political reforms and the rule of law. We focused on integrating China into the international system, ignoring clear evidence that China, under the Communist Party's leadership, would play by its own rules.

China has not become a "responsible stakeholder" in the international system as predicted. Quite the contrary, despite decades of remarkable economic growth, Beijing's leaders are increasingly dismissive of "Western influence" and hostile to both free societies and democratic capitalism.

A strategy of engagement through trade, investment, and people-to-people exchanges has not lead to a freer China and remains cold comfort to China's repressed human rights lawyers, religious and ethnic minority groups, journalists, and civil society leaders.

The U.S. must recognize that China's internal repression drives its external aggression and develop new policy approaches that intertwine our principles and interests in the pivotal Asia-Pacific region.

Working with the Congress, the next Administration should be prepared to bolster U.S. strategic advantages in the Asia-Pacific. This will mean improving military readiness, insisting on freer and fairer trade, strengthening relations with regional partners, and making more robust commitments to advancing democratic institutions, human rights, and the rule of law.

This last point will require the U.S. to push China to embrace greater transparency and better adherence to universal standards. It will require the next Administration to shine a bright light on human rights abuses and level meaningful sanctions in response to these abuses. The U.S. must also find ways to support China's reformers, dissidents, and its champions of liberty and the rule of law.

The bipartisan Congressional-Executive Commission on China (CECC), which we cochair, recently issued its 2016 Annual Report with specific recommendations for ways to pursue human rights and the rule of law within U.S.-China relations.

This report is the "gold standard" of human rights reports on China. I want to publicly commend the CECC staff for their efforts producing the report. It is a big task and I appreciate their hard work. The report should be required reading for Members of Congress interested in China, journalists writing on China, and for Administration officials looking to develop strategies to engage with China.

The need for principled and consistent American leadership is more important than ever, as China's growing economic clout, and persistent diplomatic efforts, have succeeded in dampening global criticism of its escalating repression and failures to adhere to universal standards.

We owe a new approach to Liu Xiaobo, Li Heping, and the thousands of other suffering prisoners of conscience. And, we owe it to future generations of Americans, whose security and prosperity will depend on a U.S.-China relationship that is open and transparent, free of censorship and persecution, based in adherence to universal standards and, hopefully; increasingly democratic.

68

PREPARED STATEMENT OF HON. MARCO RUBIO, A U.S. SENATOR FROM FLORIDA;
COCHAIRMAN, CONGRESSIONAL-EXECUTIVE COMMISSION ON CHINA

DECEMBER 7, 2016

Thank you Chairman Smith and thank you to all of the witnesses gathered here today—this is an impressive group of men and women who have important stories to share about their own personal suffering and that of their family members and associates at the hands of the Chinese government and Communist Party. Their experiences must not be viewed in isolation, rather they are representative of untold numbers of other Chinese, Tibetans and Uyghurs who daily face repression. Today I joined Rep. Smith in sending a letter to the Chinese Ambassador to raise our concern and seek additional information about a spate of detentions involving prominent Chinese human rights advocates, as well American citizen Sandy Phan-Gillis who has been arbitrarily detained for twenty-one months now—I submit a copy of that correspondence for the Record.

Before going any further, I'd like to take a moment at this hearing, the last CECC hearing of the 114th Congress, to recognize Chairman Smith for his capable and principled leadership of the Commission. He is an unrelenting advocate for human rights and rule of law in China and around the globe and I look forward to continuing to partner with him in the new Congress—because as today's testimony will no doubt make clear, the mandate and mission of this Commission is as vital as ever.

The Commission's recently released Annual Report painted an undeniably bleak picture regarding the deterioration of human rights and the rule of law in China, with especially grave consequences for civil society, religious believers, human rights lawyers, and labor activists. Since the Report's release in October 2016, those abuses have continued apace in the last two months.

As the Report documents and as new stories from the last several weeks underscore, Beijing has become increasingly brazen in exerting its extraterritorial reach. This was especially true in the outrageous abductions of the Hong Kong booksellers last year—including Swedish national Gui Minhai who is still being held by Chinese authorities at an undisclosed location—and now more recently in China's unprecedented intervention in Hong Kong's legal system in the cases surrounding two democratically elected politicians who won seats in the Legislative Council on platforms calling for democratic self-determination for Hong Kong. The ripple effects of this ruling are not fully known yet as the Hong Kong government has now taken additional steps targeting opposition lawmakers. This is gravely concerning and something which the Commission, and the Congress, will be watching closely in the coming year especially as it relates to the Hong Kong Policy Act.

Returning to the focus of today's hearing, we are at a critical juncture in U.S.-China relations, and there is much wisdom to be gleaned, for the incoming administration, from dissident voices.

December will mark fifteen years since China gained entry to the World Trade Organization. It is past time to take stock of our approach and recognize that despite what proponents at the time believed would happen, China has in fact used the international rules-based system to fuel vast economic growth, while further restricting freedom and increasing repression. Quite simply, many of the principles which have undergirded U.S.-China relations during Democrat and Republican administrations alike in recent decades have not yielded the desired outcomes.

A perennial critique from those who care about human rights issues has been that the U.S. foreign policy apparatus risks ghettoizing human rights concerns, only giving them the prominence they merit during infrequent, and often ineffective, human rights dialogues and then relegating these issues to the sidelines in high-level bilateral engagement.

The Obama administration struggled to integrate human rights issues at the highest levels sending unmistakable signals early on, as was famously reported during then Secretary Clinton's inaugural trip to China in 2009 that human rights issues, quote, "can't interfere with the global economic crisis, the global climate change crisis and the security crisis." Words have consequences, midlevel appointees at the State Department and elsewhere take them to heart. As such, it will be critical, during the early days of the new administration, for the Secretary and other senior diplomats to put down markers on these issues which are of central import not only to the Chinese people, but to U.S. national interests. For as history has shown us, where rule of law fails to take root, where human rights abuses are committed with impunity, where international obligations are violated, the U.S. should not expect to find a responsible global stakeholder.

I look forward to hearing from our witnesses on this important topic. Today's hearing was scheduled to coincide with the commemoration of Human Rights Day this weekend, and also with the sixth anniversary of the awarding of the Nobel Peace Prize to Chinese dissident and writer Liu Xiaobo—an honor he has not been able to rightfully claim given that still today he languishes unjustly in prison, serving an eleven-year sentence handed down for his essays criticizing the Chinese government.

The U.S. must commit anew to standing with China's reformers and dissidents, embracing their aspirations and consistently pressing the Chinese Government and Communist Party to respect basic human rights and uphold the rule of law. I look forward to today's testimony and policy recommendations.

70

SUBMISSIONS FOR THE RECORD

STATEMENT SUBMITTED FOR THE RECORD BY ENGHEBATU TOGOCHOG, OF THE
SOUTHERN MONGOLIAN HUMAN RIGHTS INFORMATION CENTER (SMHRIC)

DECEMBER 7, 2016

Dear Chairperson Christopher Smith, Co-Chair Marco Rubio and distinguished
members of the Commission,

It is my great honor to have this opportunity to bring to your attention the deteriorating human rights conditions and worsening humanitarian crisis in the Mongolian areas in China.

14 years ago, on August 5, 2002, on behalf of the Southern Mongolian Human
Rights Information Center (SMHRIC), I testified before the Commission and
brought to the attention of the Commission the specific human rights violation cases
including the cases of political prisoners Mr. Hada, Mr.Tegexi and the Chinese authorities' state-sponsored forced displacement of Mongolian herders from their ancestral lands.

We are truly grateful to the Commission for its great effort in the past 14 years
to raise public awareness of human rights issues of the Mongolian people by including a great deal of information we provided into the Commission's annual reports
as well as updating its political prisoner database with the cases of Mongolian dissidents and activists who have been arrested, detained and imprisoned by the Chinese authorities for promoting and defending their basic human rights and fundamental freedoms.

Yet, 14 years later today, human rights situations of the Mongolian people in
China have gone from bad to worse. Mr. Hada, President of the Southern Mongolian
Democratic Alliance, is still under house arrest in an apartment owned and guarded
by the Inner Mongolia Autonomous Region Public Security authorities, after serving
the full term of 15 years imprisonment and an additional 4-year extrajudicial detention.

Despite the Chinese authorities' cruel torture and inhumane treatment in the
past 21 years, Hada has consistently refused to admit that he committed any crime.
Recently Hada completed his written appeal to the Chinese Supreme People's Court,
demanding the Chinese authorities retry his case for the Inner Mongolia Autonomous Region Public Security authorities illegally sentencing him to 15 years in prison, holding him for another 4 years of extrajudicial detention, and maltreating and
persecuting him and his family members.

Hada's family members including Ms. Xinna and son Mr.Uiles are still under
tight surveillance and subjected to constant harassment by the Chinese Public Security and State Security authorities after spending multiple and extended period of
extrajudicial detentions for defending their rights and refusing to cooperate with the
authorities.

Xinna, was arrested on December 4, 2010, on a trumped-up charge of "involvement in illegal business," referring to her Mongolian Studies Bookstore. In April
2012, she was sentenced to three years in prison with five years reprieve on the
same charge.

In 2002, the then 17-year-old Uiles, was arrested and sentenced to two years in
prison for another trumped-up case of "involvement in robbery." On December 5,
2010, Uiles was arrested for "illegal drug possession." After nearly a year of detention, he was discharged but was placed under "residential surveillance," a form of
house arrest.

Another case we would like to highlight is the case of Ms. Huuchinhuu Govruud,
a human rights defender, dissident writer and activist. A month ago, Huuchinhuu
died of cancer at the age of 61 in her home place of Tongliao Municipality. Until
her last breath, at her deathbed she had been monitored and guarded by Chinese
State Security personnel around the clock for her "possible threat to the national
interest and state security of China."

Huuchinhuu's son, and only family member, Mr. Cheel Borjigin, himself has also
been diagnosed with brain cancer and is receiving chemotherapy in Minneapolis, the
United States. As an outspoken critic of the Chinese Government, returning to visit
his mother had been totally impossible for Cheel. His multiple requests to the Chinese Government to allow his mother to come to the United States for medical treatment have been turned down.

In early November 2010, Huuchinhuu was arrested by the Chinese authorities for
rallying the Mongolians via the Internet to cheer for the scheduled release of Hada.

After nearly two years of enforced disappearance and extrajudicial detention, Huuchinhuu was placed under house arrest in one of her relatives' residences in Tongliao Municipality. She was denied the right to communication, including by Internet, phone access and postal service.

On November 28, 2012, Huuchinhuu was tried behind closed doors and pronounced guilty by the Tongliao Municipality People's Court for "providing state secrets to a foreign organization." Since then, she has virtually been placed under indefinite house arrest.

In 2007, she was denied a passport for her "possible threat to the national interest and state security of China." Since then, her requests to visit her son in the United States and receive medical treatment abroad have consistently been rejected by the Chinese authorities.

Mr. Chairman, over the past 14 years, hundreds other Mongolian dissidents, activists and writers have been arrested, detained, sent to jail and placed under house arrest for expressing their political views, promoting and protecting freedom of speech, freedom of press and freedom of assembly.

In addition to these cases of Mongolian political prisoners, dissidents and activists, here I would like to turn to the worsening humanitarian crisis unfolded in rural Mongolian communities as a direct result of the Chinese authorities' intensifying economic exploitation, resource extraction, cultural eradication and environmental destruction in Mongolian areas. The very survival of the Mongolians as a distinct people is threatened. Their right to maintain their traditional way of life, and their right to access their land, water and other resources are completely denied. The Mongolians who maintained their pastoralist way of life for thousands of years are now forced by the Chinese authorities to give up their traditional life-style to give way to expanding Chinese encroachment.

Since 2001, the Chinese government has implemented the so-called "Ecological Migration" policy in rural Mongolian pastoralist communities. This policy was officially instituted to forcibly relocate the entire Mongolian pastoralist population from their ancestral grazing lands to the predominantly Chinese populated agricultural and urban areas in the name of "protecting the grassland eco-system" and "improving the living standard of rural communities."

Another policy adopted for the purpose of putting an end to the Mongolian traditional way life was the "Livestock Grazing Ban" (or "jin mu"). Under this policy, Mongolian herders grazing livestock on their own pastures were considered criminals and subjected to large fines or confiscation of their livestock.

Mr. Chair, when I testified before the Commission in 2002, these policies were just adopted. 14 years later today, these policies achieved their determined goal with the desired outcome: putting to an end to the millennia-old nomadic civilization within the borders of China.

According to a statement posted on May 30, 2012 on the official website of the Central People's Government of the People's Republic of China, the State Council Steering Committee meeting hosted by Chinese Premier Wen Jiabao passed the "Twelfth Five-Year Plan for the Project on Resettling Nomadic People within China." The announcement marks a major and seemingly final step toward eliminating the remaining population of nomad herders and eradicating the thousands of years old nomadic way of life in China.

According to the statement, the Twelfth Five-Year Plan aimed to resettle the remaining nomad population of 246,000 households or 1.157 million nomads by the end of 2015. The socio-economic and political purposes of the plan were stated "to accelerate the development mode shift of animal husbandry and grassland eco-system protection in pastoralist areas, to maintain ethnic harmony and frontier stability, and to lay a firm foundation for building an all around prosperous society."

Another earlier statement posted on August 3, 2011 on the Chinese State Council website states that the Chinese Ministry of Finance allocated a special fund of 1.7 billion Yuan to the project of resettling nomadic herders particularly in "Xinjiang (including Xinjiang Development Corps), Inner Mongolia and Tibet."

With the Mongolian out, now it is time for the Chinese to be in. In 2009, the Chinese Central Government announced in that the Mongolian regions became the largest "energy base of China." Chinese extractive industries immediately started to rush to the Mongolian grasslands to open up coal, gas, oil, and other minerals, not only destroying the natural environment, but also escalating the tension between the Chinese and the Mongolians.

Tensions have escalated between the Mongolian herders and the Chinese authorities as clashes took place almost on a daily basis. In 2011, the brutal killing of a Mongolian herder named Mergen by a Chinese mining truck sparked a large-scale, region-wide protest by Mongolian herders and students. Chinese authorities mobilized the People's Liberation Army and large numbers of police forces to crackdown on the protest.

Since then violent clashes have been widespread between Mongolian herders, who are attempting to defend their land, and Chinese miners, who open up mines recklessly to destroy the grassland for profit. Defending the interest of the Chinese miners and settlers, Chinese authorities are using excessive force, including police and prison system to crack down on the Mongolians. Many herders who defended their land and demand justice have been assaulted, injured, hospitalized, arrested, detained, and sent to jail.

As a result of large-scale unregulated mining, unscrupulous resource extraction and uncontrolled agricultural practices by the Chinese, Mongolian grassland ecosystem has seriously been destroyed; lakes and rivers are dried up; underground water is depleted; air and water is heavily polluted; the Mongolians herders who have been kicked out of their land have become landless and homeless on their ancestral land.

In response to these humanitarian crisis and environmental destruction, Mongolian herders are standing up to defend their right to survival. In the past year alone nearly 80 major protest and clashes are reported, and no less than 1000 herders have been arrested, detained, and sent to jail for defending their land.

We ask the Commission to continue to pay closer attention to the development of deteriorating human rights situations and deepening humanitarian crisis in the Mongolian areas of China, and pressure the Chinese Government to take a prompt action to prevent the situations from becoming worse.

Thank you.

Enghebatu Togochog

ONE HUNDRED FOURTEENTH CONGRESS
REPRESENTATIVE CHRISTOPHER H. SMITH, CHAIRMAN
SENATOR MARCO RUBIO, COCHAIRMAN

December 7, 2016

His Excellency Cui Tiankai
Ambassador of the People's Republic of China to the United States
3505 International Place, NW
Washington, DC 20008

Dear Ambassador Cui:

We write to express our deep concern regarding the recent disappearances of three Chinese citizens—Jiang Tianyong (江天勇), Liu Feiyue (刘飞跃), Huang Qi (黄琦)—and ask that you provide us with information about their whereabouts and any charges that they face. We urgently seek information regarding their detentions, which appear to be arbitrary, and therefore in violation of international human rights standards.

Jiang Tianyong, a former lawyer disbarred in 2009 for his representation of members of various religious groups and rights advocates including Chen Guangcheng, disappeared on November 21, 2016, when he was returning to Beijing from Changsha, Hunan, where he visited the wife of lawyer Xie Yang, one of many legal professionals detained during a nationwide crackdown that began around July 2015. Police in Hunan and Beijing respectively declined to open an investigation into Jiang's disappearance, and denied the family's request to release surveillance video recordings of the train station where Jiang was believed to have disappeared.

On November 17, 2016, police from Suizhou, Hubei, detained Liu Feiyue, founder and editor of a human rights' website known as Civil Rights & Livelihood Watch (民生观察), and raided his home. A source close to Liu reported that police told his family that he may be charged with "subversion of state power" for allegedly receiving foreign funding. Police have not provided the family with a detention notice and have refused to disclose the location of Liu's detention.

In the evening of November 28, 2016, Huang Qi, founder and editor of a human rights' website known as 64 Tianwang (64 天网), was taken away from his home in Chengdu, Sichuan, by authorities. Huang Qi's detention is particularly troubling in light of Reporters Without Borders' announcement in early November that it selected 64 Tianwang as one of the recipients of its 2016 Press Freedom prize. In addition, Huang's 83 year-old mother Pu Wenqing is also reported missing after she told reporters that that police had forcibly entered her home and detained her in a guesthouse. Radio Free Asia reported on December 5, 2016, that a local source in China alleges that Ms. Pu has been incommunicado for more than 100 hours.

As of the date of this letter, there is no public information available detailing the whereabouts of Liu, Jiang, and Huang, and their families have not been provided with a written notice about their detentions or charges being lodged against them. The immediate disclosure of information concerning detention is consistent with the National Human Rights Action Plan recently published by your government's State Council.

The fact that the three individuals were taken into custody by authorities from different provinces during a short time period makes it seem that such efforts were coordinated, not unlike the crackdown that began around July 2015 in which over 300 legal professionals and rights advocates were detained or disappeared.

The continued detentions without trial of lawyers and rights defenders including Li Heping, Xie Yanyi, Wang Quanzhang, and Wu Gan, is gravely concerning as is the case of American citizen Sandy Phan-Gillis, who has been arbitrarily detained now for the last twenty-one months.

The need for stronger and better bilateral relations is something we, as Chairs of the Congressional-Executive Commission on China and senior members of the House Foreign Affairs Committee and Senate Foreign Relations Committee respectively, are committed to pursuing but not at the expense of basic human rights protections and rule of law advances. As the U.S. Government transitions to a new Administration in the coming weeks, these glaring violations stand out as part of a larger pattern that needlessly complicates bilateral relations. We look forward to your response and ongoing interaction moving forward.

Sincerely,

Congressman Chris Smith
Chairman

Senator Marco Rubio
Cochair

DISSIDENTS WHO HAVE SUFFERED FOR HUMAN RIGHTS IN CHINA:
A LOOK BACK AND A LOOK FORWARD

DECEMBER 7, 2016

Witness Biographies

Chen Guangcheng, Chinese legal advocate; Distinguished Visiting Fellow, Institute for Policy Research and Catholic Studies, Catholic University

Mr. Chen Guangcheng is a Chinese legal advocate and activist. Mr. Chen is from rural China, where he advocated on behalf of people with disabilities, and exposed and challenged abuses of population planning officials, including forced abortions and sterilizations. Mr. Chen was imprisoned for his activism for four years. Following an additional two years of extrajudicial confinement at his home, Mr. Chen escaped in 2012 and came to the United States with his family. His courageous escape from China is detailed in his 2015 memoir, "The Barefoot Lawyer: A Blind Man's Fight for Justice and Freedom in China." In addition to his position at the Catholic University, Mr. Chen is also a Senior Distinguished Advisor to the Lantos Foundation for Human Rights and Justice.

Penpa Tsering, Representative of His Holiness the Dalai Lama, Office of Tibet, Washington, DC

Mr. Penpa Tsering is the Representative of the Office of Tibet in Washington, DC. He was born in 1967 in Bylakuppe, south India and is a member of the Tibetan Parliament. He studied at the Central School for Tibetans, Bylakuppe, and topped the merit list in Class XII. He graduated with an Economics Major from the Madras Christian College, Chennai. During his student days, he served as the General Secretary of both the Tibetan Freedom Movement and Nigerian Tibet Friendship Association. Later he served as the General Secretary of the Central Executive Committee of Do-mey. He then worked as the Executive Director at the Tibetan Parliamentary and Research Centre in New Delhi from 2001–2008 before being sworn in as the speaker of the 14th Tibetan Parliament in 2008. Penpa Tsering was elected to the 12th, 13th, and 14th Tibetan Parliament-in-Exile. He was elected as the Speaker of the 14th Tibetan Parliament-in-Exile with Mr Karma Choephel on 31 May 2006. During the 15th Tibetan Parliament-in-Exile in 2011, he again held the Speaker's post.

Yang Jianli, President, Initiatives for China/Citizen Power for China

Dr. Yang Jianli is President of Initiatives for China/Citizen Power for China. Dr. Yang is a scholar and democracy activist internationally recognized for his efforts to promote democracy in China. He has been involved in the pro-democracy movement in China since the 1980s and was forced to flee China in 1989 after the Tiananmen Square massacre. He holds Ph.Ds in mathematics from the University of California at Berkeley and in political economy and government from Harvard University's Kennedy School of Government. In 2002, Dr. Yang returned to China to support the labor movement and was imprisoned by Chinese authorities for espionage and illegal entry. Following his release in 2007, he founded Initiatives for China, a non-governmental organization that promotes China's peaceful transition to democracy. In March 2010, Dr. Yang co-chaired the Committee on Internet Freedom at the Geneva Human Rights and Democracy Summit.

Bob Fu, Founder and President, ChinaAid Association

Pastor Bob Fu was a leader in the 1989 student democracy movement in Tiananmen Square and later became a house church pastor. In 1996, authorities arrested and imprisoned Pastor Fu and his wife for their work. After their release, they escaped to the United States and, in 2002, he founded the ChinaAid Association. ChinaAid monitors and reports on religious freedom in China and provides a forum for discussion among experts on religion, law, and human rights in China. Pastor Fu is frequently interviewed by media outlets around the world and has testified at U.S. congressional hearings. He has also appeared before the European Parliament and the United Nations. Pastor Fu holds a double bachelor's degree from People's University and the Institute of Foreign Relations, and he has taught at the Central Party School in Beijing. In the United States, he earned a master's degree from Westminster Theological Seminary, where he is now working on his Ph.D.

Wei Jingsheng, Chairman, Overseas Chinese Democracy Coalition

Mr. Wei Jingsheng is a long-time leader of the opposition against the Chinese Communist dictatorship. He was sentenced to jail twice for a total of more than 18 years due to his democracy activism, including a groundbreaking and well-publicized essay he wrote in 1978: "The Fifth Modernization—Democracy." He is a winner of numerous human rights awards and the author of the book "The Courage to Stand Alone—Letters from Prison and Other Writings." After his exile to the United States in 1997, he founded and has been the chairman of the Overseas Chinese Democracy Coalition which is an umbrella organization for many Chinese democracy groups, with members in dozens of countries. He is also the president of both the Wei Jingsheng Foundation and the Asia Democracy Alliance.

Wang Xiaodan (Danielle Wang), Falun Gong practitioner and daughter of former political prisoner Wang Zhiwen

Ms. Wang Xiaodan was born in Beijing, China. Danielle Wang began practicing the exercise and meditation system Falun Gong in her youth with her father, Wang Zhiwen. In 1998, she moved to America for her studies and the following year the Chinese Communist Party began its persecution of Falun Gong practitioners. This put her father in prison and set her on the path of calling for help in hopes of rescuing him for the next 17 years. He was released in 2014, but was denied exit from China when Danielle and her husband attempted to bring him to the United States in August 2016.

Rebiya Kadeer, President, World Uyghur Congress

Ms. Rebiya Kadeer is a prominent human rights advocate and leader of the Uyghur people. She is the mother of 11 children, and a former laundress turned millionaire. She spent six years in a Chinese prison for standing up to the authoritarian Chinese government. Before her arrest in 1999, she was a well-known Uyghur businesswoman and at one time among the wealthiest individuals in the People's Republic of China. Ms. Kadeer has been actively campaigning for the human rights of the Uyghur people since her release from prison in 2005. She has been nominated for the Nobel Peace Prize several times since 2006. Despite Chinese government efforts to discredit her, Ms. Kadeer remains the pro-democracy Uyghur leader and heads the World Uyghur Congress, which represents the collective interest of Uyghurs around the world.